ep sport

Bowls

ep sport

Bowls

Chris Mills

A & C Black · London

First published 1987 by
A & C Black (Publishers) Limited
35 Bedford Row, London WC1R 4JH

© 1987 Chris Mills

ISBN 0 7136 5585 2

Mills, Chris, 1944-
    EP sport bowls.
    1.Bowling on the green.
    I.Title
    796.31   GV909

    ISBN 0-7136-5585-2

Printed and bound in Great Britain by
R. J. Acford, Chichester

Photography
*All photographs by kind
permission of* Bowls International.

CONTENTS

INTRODUCTION

There is ample evidence to suggest that games of a similar nature to bowls are among the oldest played by the inhabitants of many countries throughout the world. People have certainly played games with some sort of ball from very early times. These probably involved either throwing or rolling a ball at a fixed or moveable target. Historians, and many bowls enthusiasts, have argued about the authenticity of the game's origins. Like many sports, certain 'legends' have grown up around bowls, particularly the one concerning Drake's famous game at Plymouth Hoe before the Armada and those surrounding the origins of 'bias'.

It is likely that the first bowls games had many similarities to skittles and in early times were enjoyed by the English nobility. So much so, that acts were invoked to curtail these pleasures because of the adverse effect they might have on archery practice. Since archery was the country's main line of defence at the time it was obviously a serious matter.

What part bowls actually played in the run-up to the Armada is a matter of folklore, but Drake's game is still one of the most famous of matches and many schoolchildren's introduction to the sport. Even William Shakespeare made reference to bowls in his plays. For example, in *The Taming of the Shrew* he says, 'Well forward, forward! Thus the bowl should run, and not unfairly against the bias.' This line would seem to indicate that bowls had seen a dramatic structural change and were now capable of producing a curved path to their target. It is probably this fact that determined the split between the skittles-type of game, where the balls are round and are thrown directly at their target, and bowls proper in which the balls are delivered on a curved path and have a built-in bias.

By the end of the eighteenth century the game seemed to have fallen into disrepute. Most of the greens built in the fashionable areas of London in particular were soon covered by houses and so bowls became a game of the back-alleys associated with gambling. The Scots, however, were responsible for the sport's revival towards the end of the nineteenth century. They had been experimenting with the use of sea-washed turf to construct the playing surface of a green and this proved far superior to its predecessors.

In 1848 a Glasgow solicitor, William Mitchell, drew up a standard bowls code which formed the foundation for the modern game. In fact, today's rules show very little difference from those drawn up by Mitchell and later adopted by the Scottish Bowling Association when it was formed in 1892. These rules were subsequently adopted, with variations, by the English, Irish and Welsh associations, and later by the International Bowling Board which governs the game worldwide.

Bowls history would not be complete without some reference to the legendary Dr W. G. Grace. His considerable exploits on the cricket field during the latter part of the nineteenth century and the early 1900s have often obscured the fact that he was also an international bowler and the first president of the English Bowling Association. His reputation grew in the Victorian age, even when there was no great publicity machinery to build his image: his fame stemmed from his ability to achieve outstanding feats in sport.

Having left his native Gloucestershire in 1899, the year in which he played his last matches for his county and England, he came to London to manage a new cricket team based at Crystal Palace. It was here he also turned to bowls—both outdoor and indoor. So, although better known for his cricketing exploits, within the bowls world 'W.G.' holds a special place for his work in giving impetus to the modern game, especially the international series which first took place in London in 1903 and which is still a regular highlight of the bowling calendar.

Since that time the game has expanded: in 1966 came the introduction of a World Bowls Championship in which 16 countries took part; the fifth World Championship took place at Aberdeen, Scotland, in 1984, and involved 22 countries. Now some of the magical moments of the sport are being captured on television. With this increasing interest has come more coverage in the press and certainly added interest from the general public, resulting in more and more people taking up the game.

From this it is obvious that bowls is undergoing some impressive changes, not least because of the marked interest shown by the younger generation. The days when bowls was regarded as purely a pastime for the elderly have long since gone, and today youth play a major part in the continuing expansion of the sport.

So, perhaps the first thing we should do is to begin by dispensing with the myth that has surrounded the game for a long time. Bowls is no longer an 'old man's game'. It is best to consider it as a young

BBC Sports commentator, David Vine, talks to bowls comedian, Roy Kinnear, and his celebrity pairs partner, David Bryant (left). Behind him are snookerman, Rex Williams (left), and his partner, an England International, John Bell (right).

At 18 John Dunn of Tonbridge was the youngest winner of the English Indoor Bowling Association's Singles title.

person's sport in which older players can also take part. It will, however, always be true that a vast number of bowlers will be senior citizens, simply because it is one of the few sports still open to people of advancing years.

And that is one of its greatest selling points—you can play bowls virtually from the cradle to the grave.

WHERE TO START

There are many ways by which you can be introduced to a sport. You may be persuaded by relatives or friends, you may carry on from school, you may see it on television or you may watch others in your local park. Whatever the reason, it is highly likely that whoever introduces you will be an enthusiast who will try to convert you.

Bowls is no different from many sports. Go along to any local green and engage a bowler in conversation and it will not be long before he has suggested that you 'come and join us'. Providing that it is not a serious match, it is highly likely that you will be invited to have a go there and then.

Equipment

When contemplating taking up a sport you will need to know what equipment is required and, most importantly, its cost. One of the many plus factors for bowls is that initially you can often borrow equipment, and even obtain good second-hand bargains, to start you on your way. This, and the fact that you do not need much equipment to play, makes bowls an easy sport to pursue.

Although it has two specific seasons in the UK—outdoor, usually from the beginning of May to the end of September, and indoor, from October to the end of April—the equipment is the same for both, apart from waterproof and all-weather clothing which is obviously superfluous to indoor requirements.

A pair of soft-soled, flat bowls shoes and a set of bowls (for flat green it is always best to have a set of four) are usually all you will need to play the game. Mats and jacks are normally provided by the club you join. When you decide to play on a regular basis you can go to the expense of kitting yourself out completely with such accessories as waterproofs and a measure.

It is always best to experiment as much as you can with a variety of bowls to determine what type, size and make you require and to try to seek expert advice, preferably from a club coach, on what is best

More and more youngsters are coming into the game and it is with the guidance of the older and experienced players that they will progress.

for you. The type of equipment and how to select it are dealt with in full in the next chapter.

Basic skills

The mechanics of the game will slowly unfold in the ensuing chapters but one point to remember here is that bowls *is a simple game*. Unlike many other sports where it is quite difficult to master the strokes—as in tennis and golf—bowls is a game at which most people can achieve fairly quickly a good enough standard to enjoy playing.

Basically, the game is easy to grasp, but it is essential that the beginner should start off in the correct manner. A new player

should be instructed on the equipment (bowls, mat and jack), how to place the mat, how to hold the bowl, stance on the mat, how to deliver the bowl, and so on.

It has often happened in the past (and to some extent it still does happen) that a new player was told quite simply that 'the big rings are on the outside and the little ones on the inside', and was just expected to 'get on with it' by following other players. Now, with the ever-increasing importance of coaching, most new bowlers can receive the best advice right from the start. The main objective is to ensure that all faults which may occur are eliminated from the earliest possible moment.

By having a scheme which is controlled by a central body, one can also achieve uniformity of coaching because the beginner will often imitate the person who gives him his early tuition. So, it is important that those who put novices through their preliminary paces are properly certificated and well versed in the fundamentals of good play. Wrong tuition or advice early on can produce poor players and club members.

The first season in any bowler's life is very important, and should essentially be one of training and observation. Certain basic principles have to be instilled in the mind of the new player, who could do no worse than study the Laws of the Game while mastering the art of bowling.

To say at this stage that the basic object of the game is to get your bowls nearer to the jack than your opponent's is, perhaps, an over-simplification, but you will quickly learn that 'drawing' to the jack is the most fundamental aspect of bowls. The mastery of this shot is the basis on which champions are made.

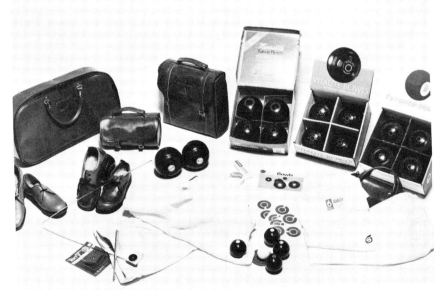

Some of the equipment available to bowlers—bowls, bags, measures, shoes, polish and, for outdoor bowling, the inevitable wet-gear.

11

The draw shot is one of a number in the bowler's range which, during the following pages, will be explained as part of the mechanics of playing. The basic skills and more advanced techniques of the game will then be explored. After this the player will be given an insight into the tactics involved with playing, how to prepare for matches and ways to perfect his game with practice.

What will be seen is that bowls provides more healthy exercise than it is often given credit for: there is the stimulation of competition and the element of comradeship in team games, and it

is also a sport in which all ages and both sexes can compete on level terms. There are few sports about which that final statement can be made!

Those are just some of the virtues of bowls and reasons for its continued expansion. In this book we will be dealing mainly with the skills required to play the game, but it must be added that many people also derive much pleasure from administrating the sport. The amount of work which numerous tireless officials undertake would probably worry even the most ardent 'workaholic'; however, without these conscientious officials the game really would come to a halt. In many cases the task of running a club falls on those who can devote the considerable amount of time needed, and often the qualities of drive, enthusiasm and knowledge of the game enable officials to exert the most influence on a club.

It is understandable if you would just like to be a player and do not care for these additional responsibilities, but always remember when you criticise that the individual concerned is only trying to do his best.

Perfect your techniques, enjoy your sport, help to support your club and you will probably find that the rewards you gain are not only measured in the trophies that hopefully will come your way at prize presentation time.

Opposite—*Coaching is a vital aspect of today's modern game. Here England's National coach, Jimmy Davidson, is seen assisting former Scottish International, Willie Adrain, in a session with some young hopefuls.*

1 EQUIPMENT AND PLAYING AREA

You have now had a few roll-ups, and even, perhaps, the odd game. So now it is decision time—do you want to play bowls? I am sure that your answer will be 'Yes', and that the next question will be, 'How do I set myself up?'

CLUBS

There should be no difficulty in finding a bowling green, with its associated club, in your district. You will probably get an idea of what a club is like simply by watching. It may be that you already know someone there who can make the introductions, but the person you should seek out is the club secretary. You are going to have to talk to him at some stage anyway, so why not straight away? The club secretary will tell you how the club's application system works: this should not take too long providing the club does not have an extensive waiting list.

Bowlers are very friendly people, and usually new members are quickly made welcome and made

to feel at ease. Remember one important point: don't be worried about being among experienced bowlers. You won't be thought foolish—they had to start once, after all! It is like everything else, you are bound to make mistakes at first, and even experienced bowlers have bowled a 'wrong bias' on odd occasions.

EQUIPMENT

You can carry on for a long time with borrowed equipment, but eventually you will no doubt want your own. As with most games there are some essentials and other items which are useful, but not always a prime requirement, and which you could get along without for a while.

Bowls

Firstly, you are obviously going to need a set of bowls (whether it be two or four) and a pair of bowls shoes. I am not going to extol the virtues of any particular make; I know which bowls I prefer (and in

some cases it is a matter of having different types and makes for different situations), but in the end you have to make your own choice. I will, however, give you some *general* advice on how to select the bowls you require and I am sure your club or county coach, if available, will be only too happy to give his valuable opinion. The best way is to try out a few makes and sizes to see what suits your particular requirements.

Many textbooks suggest that you should choose your bowls set by following a manufacturer's gauge, which determines the size of bowl in relation to the size of your hand, or by spanning the circumference of the bowl with both hands. In the latter case, the largest bowl suitable is the one around which the tips of your middle fingers just meet. However, a large school of opinion would dismiss both methods, including David Bryant and national coach, Jimmy Davidson, who both use bowls larger than a gauge would indicate. They maintain that they can handle their preferred bowls and, as both of them have each won many major titles, who would argue? There is always a danger on outdoor greens in wet weather that a bowl can be difficult to cope with, but under most conditions the bigger bowls are always an advantage.

Here are some names to ask for: **Henselite**, Australian manufactured bowls used by most players today (Henselite also produce the Almark bowls range at their Scottish factory); **Thomas Taylor's**, a famous name in bowling whose company is based in Glasgow and which produces bowls for both flat and crown green with the 'Lignoid' trademark (it also makes the David Bryant 'Drakelite' bowl); **Gray's** of Cambridge manufacture the 'Concorde'; **Vitalite** (now called **Crystalate**) are a company which also manufacture billiard, snooker and pool balls; **John Jaques**, a British firm that have been well established for many years and which produce the 'Eclipse' bowl; **Drake's Pride**, the name for crown and flat bowls manufactured by E. A. Clare of England. **A. F. Ayres** of Liverpool manufacture the modestly priced 'Green Master' bowl.

Costs vary, of course—you can pay a great deal of money for a new

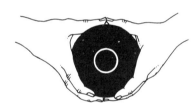

It is very important for a new bowler coming into the game to choose a set of bowls that best suits him. Although there are differing theories, most people feel that the bowl should be related to the size of your hand. Here is a simple test. Hold the bowl in both hands—you should be just able to reach round.

Right—*The unique crescent grip of the Concorde bowl follow-up to the Taylor-Rolph bowl. This would be for a right-handed player.*

set, so keep your eyes open for some good second-hand bargains. It is always advisable to buy a set of four bowls, but finances may limit you to two. Two bowls are all you will need for rink (fours) games and also for the majority of Federation games. However, singles and pairs require four bowls, except again in Federation competitions, and for triples you need three.

There is just one point to mention about the bowl. These days players talk about composition bowls, rather than 'lignums' or wooden bowls. This does not mean there are no longer any lignum sets left (and I have no doubt many older bowlers still use them, particularly on heavy outdoor greens when conditions will suit 'woods'), but now most flat green bowlers use composition bowls.

The first composition bowls appeared just before the Second World War, and have been improved tremendously since then.

'Composition', having a greater density than lignum, enables a given weight to be achieved with less material, although the actual 'mix' varies from manufacturer to manufacturer.

Now that the 'weight for size' rule has been dispensed with it means that bowlers with small hands can have a heavier weight bowl in their size. At this point it is worth quoting

the rule in the 'Laws of the Game' which governs the bowl:

'Bowls shall be made of wood, rubber or composition and shall be black or brown in colour, and each bowl of the set shall bear the member's individual and distinctive mark on each side. [This distinguishing mark only applies to international matches.] Bowls made of wood (lignum vitae) shall not exceed $16\frac{1}{2}$" in circumference, nor $3\frac{1}{2}$lb in weight.

They should bear the imprint of the stamp of the International Bowling Board, or that of the relevant national association.'

The English Indoor Bowling Association abolished the 're-stamping and testing' of bowls in 1984, and the English Bowling Association followed suit in 1985. Now only bowls used in international competitions or lignums have to be retested every 15 years. However, a new 'Master Bowl' was introduced in 1986 and bowls must now comply with this standard.

Having finally decided on your set of bowls, remembering of course that these could well last you a lifetime of bowling, you obviously need something in which to keep them. You would be amazed at the number of adaptations I have seen at bowls greens. Old suitcases, specially constructed wooden boxes, old pea-bags and even an

old pair of ladies' tights—each make suitable carriers for bowls, although many bowlers buy themselves a proper carrying case.

You can gather the various 'extras' as you go along but if you wish, and can afford to, you can acquire them straight away. A very useful, and not costly, extra is a tin of 'Grippo' polish. It has two effects on your bowls: it gives them a shine, which will ensure that they run smoothly on the green, and it also allows you to 'grip' the bowl. Again, it is very much a matter of choice. Some bowlers polish their bowls before every match and even before every bowl they play, whereas a few bowlers never bother at all.

Another item which does not cost very much is a bowls measure. There are a few different types, ranging from 3'–11' measures and telescopic measures to the old-fashioned strings. Strictly speaking, you will not need these straight away, as the number three in a game of rinks is responsible for 'measuring', and I doubt you will rise to the dizzy heights of a no. 3 for a little while.

Dress
Dress varies in different areas but often clubs insist on 'whites' above the waist. Many fixtures are played with all players dressed completely in white or 'creams', i.e. white shirt, white flannels or skirt

and pullover, with a club tie as an additional extra. When you become accustomed to all this club activity, you will accept it as just part of the camaraderie of the game—and it does give you a certain feeling of pride for your own club.

Shoes

There are a few types of bowls shoe available, including lace-ups and slip-ons. The most important point to remember is that the soles must be completely flat. You may get away with plimsolls on some public parks, but many club greenkeepers will soon be having a quiet word in your ear if you wear them on their greens. All indoor clubs will certainly insist on regulation footwear, defined in the 'Laws of the Game' as: 'brown, smooth rubber-soled heel-less shoes'.

THE GREEN

Bowling greens are usually square or at least oblong, but any piece of ground that is 40 yards long by 19 feet wide could be regarded as providing a potential bowling rink. The Laws state that 'the Green should form a square of not less than 40 yards and not more than 44 yards a side' and that it should have 'a suitable playing surface which shall be level. It should be provided with suitable boundaries in the form of a ditch and a bank.'

There are, however, many greens, both indoor and outdoor, which vary from that specification, usually by being shorter. The best greens do, of course, conform to the standards demanded by the International Bowling Board, particularly those used for national and international competitions, but there are many clubs that have to make do with smaller sized greens.

The green will be surrounded by a ditch and a bank, both of which should have surfaces which do not cause any damage to your bowls.

You will notice that the green on which you bowl is marked out, in some form or other, in sections, called rinks; usually the green will have six rinks marked out with a line of string and numbered at each end. These numbers serve a dual purpose. They obviously indicate the number of the rink, but they also serve as the centre-marker for each rink.

To start bowling you place the rubber mat 6 feet from the ditch which surrounds the green, centred on the marker. The small white ball called the **jack** (there are many local terms, such as 'kitty' and 'cot', for this important object) is rolled up the green. It must finish a minimum distance of 25 yards from the front edge of the mat and 6 feet from the back of the green, and must be centred with the marker.

The Scottish Bowling Association agreed at its 1986 Annual General Meeting to the introduction of a 70-feet minimum length jack for all matches under its jurisdiction and to 25-up shots in national singles competitions.

The new laws were adopted by the International Bowling Board at a meeting in Edinburgh in 1986, but they have been turned down by both the English and Irish associations. The Welsh association also turned down the 25-up singles plan but agreed to accept the new jack length.

Nations in the southern hemisphere, led by Australia and Fiji, regularly play to a 66-feet jack minimum and play 31-up in singles matches, whereas in the northern hemisphere, headed by the British bowling countries, a 75-feet minimum and 21-up are standard. The IBB reached the compromise laws to try to standardise the rules of bowls worldwide.

HOW TO BOWL

The most important thing to remember is that it has been a long, long time since bowls were just round balls which were rolled straight along the ground. You have what is known as a bias to contend with now. This means that the bowl is sent in an arc away from the jack. The bias comes from the inner edge of the bowl which is specially shaped to make it turn as

17

it slows in momentum. The bias side of the bowl, often marked with a set of small rings as opposed to much larger rings on the outer side, must always be on the inside as you deliver your bowl.

There are two lines that you can take to the jack, known simply as the forehand and backhand, which of course will depend on whether you are a right- or a left-handed bowler. You bowl towards the jack. The path which your bowl takes up the green is known as the *land*.

As you become more experienced you will realise that the amount of land you take will be determined by a number of variables, i.e. distance of the jack, the bias of the bowl and the state of the green.

The bowl will travel in an outward curve and then will turn inwards, approximately two-thirds of the way along its path; it will continue turning until it comes to rest. By sending a few bowls from each end of the green, you will soon be able to establish just how much land you will need to reach the jack.

Do not forget to try both your hands. It is often said that the quickest and easiest way to bowl to the jack is the forehand, but the backhand shot is a very important part of your armoury, so do not neglect it.

At this stage all you need to concentrate on is bowling to the jack. The draw shot will always remain the most important shot for any bowler, especially in singles play, so if you can master that art early on you stand a fair chance of becoming a reasonably competent bowler.

You now know about the equipment needed to start your game, you have joined the club of your choice, introduced yourself to the secretary, met other club members and played a few bowls, and so you are ready to have a game. When you were practising while first thinking about the game, you discovered a little about how

A side view of a bowl, showing the inside or biased side/small rings.

This youngster shows that despite his tender years he has already perfected a stylish delivery, even with unorthodox footwear.

to bowl. You know which side has the bias—it is one of the first basic principles—and something about how to stand on the mat. You are acquainted with forehand and backhand shots and how to take 'land'. Now is the time to put the early practice to good use.

BASIC SKILLS

GRIP

Having sorted out your equipment, you should look at some of the basics required to start playing the game—stance, delivery and the way to grip a bowl.

The size of bowl a player uses can to some degree, be affected by the grip he adopts. In bowls there are basically two ways of gripping the bowl for delivery—the **claw** and the **cradle**. A third, the 'finger' grip, is also used by some bowlers, and there are one or two other odd grips used mainly to play special shots.

As the name implies, the cradle grip is formed simply by using four fingers as the cradle and lining the thumb directly along the side of the bowl to keep it stable in the hand. So, the bowl lies in your palm, your thumb is usually below the disc and your little finger is level with the outer ring.

The cradle grip is used predominantly in the northern hemisphere where the greens are much slower and is rarely, if ever,

In the cradle grip the bowl nestles in the palm of the hand, with the thumbs placed on the side of the top running surface.

seen on the quicker surfaces of Australia and New Zealand. It has proved successful on the majority of greens but cannot be recommended for very fast surfaces, because as the bowl is palmed away it is extremely difficult to obtain the delicate touch needed under these conditions. The bowl is cradled in the palm of the hand, with the thumb approximately in the centre of the small circle or disc acting as a prop.

The claw grip is undoubtedly the most widely used as it is suitable for all conditions. The bowl is held in exactly the same way as for the cradle grip, but the thumb is placed on or slightly inside the large ring. This raises the bowl off the palm of the hand and gives a far more sensitive touch. On very fast surfaces the bowl is brought still further forwards and this is known as the finger grip.

The grip, however, is an individual preference and what suits one does not necessarily suit another. Nevertheless, there are certain precedents. The fingers must remain parallel to the running surface of the bowl: while it is generally accepted that the forefinger is placed exactly in the middle, it is not always essential providing that the fingers remain parallel. What is more important is that the bowl

In the cradle grip the fingers should be evenly spread to be parallel to the running base of the bowl.

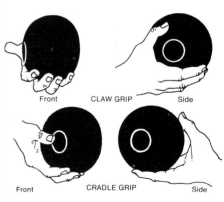

There are two main grips in bowling—the claw and the cradle. In the claw the fingers grip the bowl, while in the cradle the bowl rests in the palm of the hand.

feels comfortable in the hand, and the wrist should feel free of tension. The little finger, if incorrectly placed, can cause a wobble when delivering and the player should make sure that it does not stray too far outside the large ring.

The golden rule is to use the grip that you feel is best suited to your style—as long as you get it right!

DELIVERY

What may affect your choice of grip are your stance on the mat and the way you deliver your bowl. It is as well to remember that the first step towards successful bowling is perfecting your delivery. It is also important to realise that 'delivery' is not one distinct action. It takes in everything that you do from the moment you pick up your bowl and step on the mat to the point at which your bowl is half-way up the green.

Basically, it comprises three elements—stance, delivery and follow-through.

Stance

As with other aspects of the game, the position a player adopts on the mat, his stance, is a matter of personal preference. There is only one law which must be followed, this being that at the moment of delivery, when the bowl touches the surface of play, at least all of one foot must either be on the mat or

A back view of the athletic stance, just prior to the commencement of the delivery.

directly above it (i.e. entirely within the confines of the mat).

More experienced bowlers will work out what they feel is their best position on the mat, but for beginners it is best to start by standing in the centre, with feet parallel, a few inches apart, and pointing along the line that your bowl is going to take.

In all sports where an object has to be rolled, bowled, thrown or struck, the motive force should be generated more by weight transfer than by arm movement. In general terms the arm is a passive vehicle. Bowls is not a game that demands violent physical actions, and it is important that your delivery be conditioned to ensure a smooth and accurate line for your bowl, with a good distribution of forces on the muscles that will be used.

There are three stances which can be adopted for delivery—the athletic, the crouch and the fixed.

The *athletic* delivery, often known as the upright stance, is easily the most popular and is seen on greens throughout the world. It certainly proves an advantage on slower greens as it is far easier to impart more force behind the bowl and still maintain accuracy from this position than from any other.

The *crouch* delivery, although not as common as the athletic, is a generally accepted alternative

The crouch stance for delivery—a personal choice for David Bryant. He feels that it enables him to maintain a more accurate line.

and is used by quite a large number of players. Some players adopt this stance because they believe it enables them to maintain a more accurate line. However, other factors such as a player's height, weight, reach and leg length have to be considered.

The *fixed* delivery is the least used and is often adopted by bowlers with a physical disability, because it is the most comfortable way for them to ground the bowl.

Selecting the initial stance is entirely up to the individual player, the main criteria being that he feels comfortable and at ease on the mat. The feet should be sufficiently wide apart to give a good balance, the knees should be relaxed and the body weight should be slightly forward. The bowl should be held firmly but without tension in the wrist or arm.

As the name indicates, the upright delivery involves the bowler standing erect. The body weight is evenly balanced between the two feet, and the body is inclined slightly forwards to an extent that is comfortable for the particular individual. The weight will be more evenly spread the better the

Not everyone would adopt this very original delivery stance. Note that both hands are used to steady the bowl prior to commencement.

shoulders make a parallel line with the ground.

The bowler should be aiming for the optimum mixture of balance and comfort. The legs and knees should not be stiff but should be relaxed, and you should remember to avoid any unbalancing tilt to either side. The arm holding the bowl may be held slightly to the front but not too far forwards, and the bowler should take up a position on the mat so that his feet are pointing along the intended line of delivery. So, if he is planning delivery on the backhand, he will be facing fractionally to the left (assuming he is right-handed), while forehand shots will cause him to face to the right. If you are correctly positioned your whole body should be facing along the delivery line, with your trunk at an angle to a line drawn through the centre of the mat to the jack.

If you want to make comparisons between the two main delivery positions—the upright and the crouch—it is worth considering the physical logistics of them both. With the crouch the left step has been taken before the arm starts moving. Therefore, subsequent forward weight transfer is limited and since the knees are already bent the delivery cannot, unless an exaggerated and probably uncontrolled backswing is used, employ the force of gravity to any

The unusual semi-fixed crouch style of England Indoor international Terry Heppell. He is one of the rare players to deliver from the back of the mat.

great extent. The bulk of the required force must come from the least controllable factor, the degree of muscular contraction. The arm is no longer the passive vehicle but the mainspring.

With the upright position both the constant force factors—descent of the bowl and forward stride—are involved and are more easily adjustable. So much so that the third less predictable factor, muscular contraction, need not be used. The arm here is a passive vehicle. Clearly, from the point of view of smoothness and adjustment to all conditions, the upright stance must be preferable.

Whatever stance is used, however, it is important at this stage to examine what your objective is. The new player should understand what bias means: it is the tendency of a bowl to deviate from a straight line in movement because of an imbalance built in by shaping. This is mentioned because your position and subsequent delivery should be geared to the biasing effect of the bowl.

Aiming point

The arc that a bowl takes to reach the jack will vary according to many conditions—the state of the green, whether it is fast or slow, etc.—so it is essential that a player fixes his point of aim before delivering the bowl. Whatever the pace of the green the line, or angle, from the mat is constant for all lengths of jack.

The point at which a bowl starts turning towards the jack is called the shoulder of the arc. The player must make his aiming point slightly outside this mark for the bowl to follow a true line. As the shoulder is approximately two-thirds of the distance (some say three-fifths) between the mat and the jack, the recommended aiming point is not less than this, although the line can be extended as far as the bank. Any discolourations on the green or marks on the bank can be used as an aid to perfecting accurate lines.

As a beginner, how do you go about finding the correct amount of green to take? As a starting point, you can begin by choosing a spot on the bank to the right of the centre number-plate, assuming you are a right-handed player about to play a forehand shot. Then try to visualise a straight line running back from this point through the shoulder of the arc to the mat. This is your chosen grass-line and the line along which you should bowl, placing your feet in the same direction.

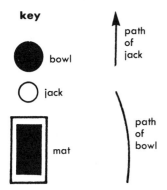

key

bowl

jack

mat

path of jack

path of bowl

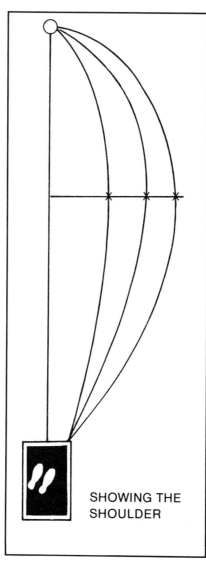

SHOWING THE
SHOULDER

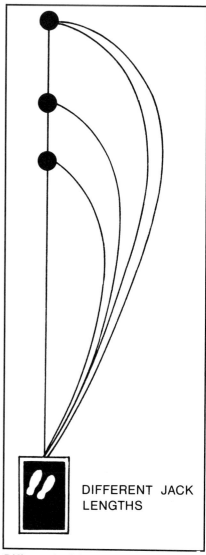

DIFFERENT JACK
LENGTHS

Showing the shoulder. *Providing the surface of a green is fairly true, the shoulder is about two-thirds of the distance from the jack on any line.*

Different jack lengths. *On a true green the initial direction of delivery should be the same for all jack lengths, but you should take a slightly wider line on longer ends, since the end of a green tends to be of a quicker pace than the middle.*

Some bowlers choose a mark near to the mat, some the actual shoulder of the arc. Don't worry about the jack, simply concentrate on delivering your bowl along the line.

If your bowl is not achieving its objective, you will need to re-examine your line. You can move your mark, visualise the new line back from it to the mat, readjust the position of your feet and bowl along the new line.

The mark that you choose on the bank, or elsewhere, is not actually used as the point at which you will play your bowl, but merely to provide the line which you should take with the bowl. If the mat is moved up the green, the angle from the mat to the mark has been increased so that the aiming point must now be on a line greater than the original. If the jack is moved off its centre-point, you will need to find another mark, move your shoulder point accordingly and bowl along the new grass-line.

So, just to summarise: the first duty of the bowler when he steps on the mat is to look at the jack to determine its distance from his intended point of delivery; then he must 'draw' his imaginary line. Estimation of this line and of the widest point of the arc the bowl will travel is very important. Once the 'shoulder' has been fixed in the mind's eye, the stance should be

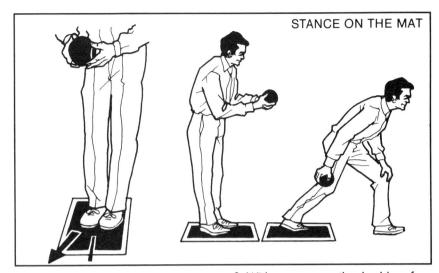

STANCE ON THE MAT

1. Choose the line you wish to take and position your feet so that they point along that line. Do not grip the bowl too firmly.

2. With your eye on the shoulder of the green, bring your arm back in a pendulum-like motion. As you do this your left foot should go forwards. Your arm will then come forwards in an easy movement.

3. The bowl is released as close to the surface of the green as possible, with the back foot either on or over the mat.

4. The bowl has been released and the arm is pointing along the line of delivery, with the fingers still in a grip position and the palm facing up. The firmer the shot, the fuller the follow-through.

27

taken along a line pointing to it. Your eyes should never leave this line and all your concentration should be applied when delivering the bowl exactly along it. Even at the moment of delivery and at the end of the follow-through your eyes should be firmly fixed on the shoulder. The reason for this is fairly simple. It is far easier to bowl at and hit the shoulder than to bowl to the arc as a whole—it is easier to bowl at something than to nothing.

A left-hander's line will naturally be different from that of a right-hander's; each is bowling on opposite hands, the right-hander's forehand being the left-hander's backhand.

Delivery
Whether you are in an upright or a crouched position, you must keep your weight back and over the leading leg.

Having fixed the line of delivery in your mind, you must now determine the weight required to get your bowl to the jack. Looking along the point of aim, 'weigh' your bowl in your hand, moving it up and down to find a correlation between the weight of the bowl and the distance it has to be bowled. To achieve a good, flowing action you need to 'weigh' the bowl well—it must 'come alive' in your hands.

On a reasonably fast green you can develop 'touch' with the bowl: it slips out of the fingers in a nice smooth, flowing delivery. On heavy greens it is more important to grip the bowl firmly, because more force has to be used in the delivery. (It is more difficult to feel length on a heavy green.)

Scotland's former Commonwealth Games Singles gold medallist, Willie Wood, is a player who uses the athletic delivery—a very helpful method on the heavier Scottish greens. It relies on a full swing of the arm, with the backfoot firmly anchored on the mat.

The bodyweight is firmly over the front foot as the arm swings forwards; the bowler's head is still while he looks down the delivery line.

A constant delivery, when the bowl is grounded perfectly each time, is essential to every bowler. While no two players appear to have an identical technique, there are certain principles to which every bowler must adhere. Firstly, from the moment he takes his stance and addresses the green the bowler's body must move rhythmically down the aiming line. During the delivery the shoulder, elbow, forearm, wrist and bowl should all remain aligned, and should move along the aiming line with a smooth, flowing action. The elbow must not be allowed to stray away from the side of the body, since this will cause a 'hooked' delivery, and neither must the wrist be allowed to twist as the bowl is grounded.

During delivery the body weight has to be transferred from the right foot to the left foot and, to enable the player to maintain a smooth action, it is recommended that the left hand is placed on the left thigh to act as a prop. This minimises any slight wobble which could result in the player missing his line.

The actual delivery is a combination of a forward step with the left foot and a pendulum-like swing of the right arm. The bowl is held in front of the body, addressing the aiming line, and as it swings back and is passing the body the left foot is raised and moves forward along the delivery line. The foot, however, does not make contact with the green until the arm has begun its forward swing. It is essential that the knees are bent and relaxed, enabling the body weight to be transferred successfully to the left foot.

The moment of delivery: the bowl, perfectly grounded, glides away from the finger-tips, with the bowler's backfoot on the mat and his eyes following the line.

The final follow-through of a slightly unorthodox but beautifully balanced delivery.

FOLLOW-THROUGH

In most ball games a smooth follow-through is an essential, and bowls is no exception. A good follow-through can only be achieved if the body weight is well forward over the front foot, which dictates that the back foot rises on to the toes or is even raised above the mat according to the power of the swing. The delivery hand will be pointing along the line; this will minimise the tendency to hook, jab or flick the bowl, which would make it difficult to control its length.

The bowler must also remember never to lift his head until the bowl has left his hand. It is natural for the body to follow the line and the back foot should be allowed to move forwards past the front one. It is a good habit to take several steps down the path of the bowl as you regain your upright position.

Practise your delivery so that it becomes second-nature: every bowl must be grounded the same way. Try bowling at a fixed-point jack; keep the same length and get four bowls to draw to the jack every time. (If you can do this your delivery must be right.) When you

Keeping your eyes along the line of delivery helps to ensure correct body weight transfer. It is demonstrated here by Brett Long, a National Outdoor Singles semi-finalist.

have mastered drawing to the jack at one particular length, try it at other lengths.

First fix your line, then your weight. If a bowler has complete confidence that his mechanics are right, he will be able to bowl under pressure; however, a nervous bowler will make mistakes. It is obviously easier to concentrate and play well on a good green, but you must be prepared to play on greens requiring different weights. Weight control is undoubtedly the most difficult part of any bowler's game, particularly as the pace of greens can be so variable.

Experienced bowlers from the northern hemisphere do not automatically adapt to the much faster surfaces in the south, and vice versa. Weight control, therefore, is a skill which is not simple to coach, although there are certain basic facts which should always be remembered.

Firstly, good weight control comes from correct propulsion. This is determined by the length of the swing. It is best to hold the bowl high for a heavy green and to use a long backswing; conversely, keep the bowl low for a fast surface and use little or no backswing.

The length of the step will also vary with the propulsion and speed of delivery, but it is best for the player to concentrate on swing rather than step, as the latter is

A perfectly smooth delivery follow-through, although with the unusual kneeling position for the right leg, from Scottish Ladies Indoor Singles Champion, Jeanette Conlan.

invariably sympathetic to the former. Try walking and taking long strides without swinging your arms, or try taking tiny steps swinging your arms!

On heavier greens a longer step and backswing will be needed, with a much faster action. If the player's action is of 'copy-book' style, with head down and hand following the line, his back foot will automatically rise above the mat. On fast greens the bowler will take a short step, use little backswing and make a slow delivery keeping as low as possible. At the same point of delivery the momentum is such that the back foot should only rise to the toes during follow-through.

3 MORE SKILLS

HOW TO APPROACH BOWLS

It is a known fact that few sports are as incorrectly approached as bowls. Too often the casual observer is persuaded to join in a match, shown the basic rudiments of the game, and then left very much to his own devices. This casual approach, while fostering friendly relations, is not really conducive to providing the right approach for a beginner.

The novice should really spend a considerable amount of time standing on the bank observing what the game is all about before he decides on, or is forced into, taking his place on the green.

The person who is not given the correct shoes, bowls or told how to stand properly on the mat is on a course of self-destruction, and unless caught within the first two or three years may never alter the bad habits that he will invariably acquire. Getting the right approach to the game is essential for all aspiring players, whether

they wish to play just for pleasure or to take the game seriously.

I have met many players in my time who have alleged 'I'm just here for fun, I don't take it seriously' and then proceeded to put bowls close to the jack every end and beaten their opponents hollow. Perhaps the best tip I was ever given came from a top international bowler who told me in an interview, 'Never trust a smiling opponent!'

In the formative stages of a player's game it is essential that the learning process should be fairly 'painless'. Nothing can frustrate a player more than to keep making the same mistakes and to find that he does not seem to be improving. That is not to say that early mistakes are not beneficial: it is often good to experience them at the start and then to find out how to make the necessary corrections.

Taking beginners out on to a green armed with jack and bowls is not necessarily the best way of introducing them to the game. To

be exposed to the gaze of players, both on and off the green, may not be the best commencement.

Whether a player is just starting, or seeking to improve or correct a fault that has crept in, he should always be given tuition in comfortable conditions. It is rather like playing in cricket-nets, which are usually sited away from the cricket pitch. They create the aura of a practice arena where mistakes are tolerated more and new techniques are actively encouraged.

A new player should undergo a 'check-up' before starting to see that he has the correct equipment and then he should be given visual demonstrations, preferably by a qualified coach or, if one is not available, by an experienced player. This initial induction will stand him in good stead when he moves out on to the green for those first tantalising steps to try to conquer the fundamental principles.

THE RIGHT TECHNIQUES

Too many players have drifted into the game and then been expected within a matter of weeks to play shots which are difficult enough for more experienced players. It is therefore essential that new players are taught to get the right type of bowl for them, to learn to hold it properly and then to adopt the correct stance for delivery. These points have all been discussed in the previous chapter, but it cannot be stressed enough just how important they are in the education of new bowlers.

Many bowlers sacrifice control by not using the correct bowl, although having said that, there are bowlers who have been considerably successful using bowls which experts would say were not suited to them. In their cases achievement has often come through perseverance and natural talent.

Top photograph sequence on pages 33-5—*The 'clinic' method of delivery is one that involves the minimum amount of movement in the action, thereby reducing the possibility of error creeping in. It was developed in South Africa by Dr Julius Sergay in 1961.*

Bottom photograph sequence on pages 33-5—*Two exponents of this style are former South African bowler, Cecil Bransky, and Welshman, Terry Sullivan, who refashioned his delivery after watching Bill Moseley on television when he appeared in the Kodak Masters.*

34

The next essential for any aspiring bowler is to perfect a suitable stance. A balanced stance is the mainspring of a bowler's delivery.

In most sports the position adopted as a preliminary for whatever action ensues is geared to provide the best result. The golfer when he tees off, the cricketer at the wicket and the snooker player about to pot: all adopt a position that will enable them to play their best shot.

In bowling there are many styles, some orthodox and others variations on a theme, but all should become second-nature and should be executed naturally.

Much has been written about the virtues of the upright stance over the crouch delivery, but it is a known fact that the upright stance provides a better balanced position, with harmonious muscular action in which the whole of the body takes part. From the preliminary address to the vital follow-through there should be one concentrated, flexible movement, with the bowl being grounded at the lowest point of the swing.

At the moment of delivery the hand should follow through in a semi-circular motion. Some players find that lifting the trailing leg (in the case of a right-hander who plays off the left foot this will be the right leg) aids balance. Many players will also place their left hand on the left knee; others follow their bowl for a few paces up the green.

One point is certain: once the bowl has left your hand there is nothing more you can do to aid its path to your objective, although the famous Scottish international skip, Harry Reston, was well-known for talking his bowls into the head. Whatever results he achieved, however, were purely because of his considerable skill.

Go through these motions as often as possible, with or without a bowl, since perfecting your delivery is the first step towards successful bowling.

ACCURACY

When a player first starts playing bowls he generally has one idea fixed in his mind—that of getting his bowls as near as possible to the jack. And that is not a bad aim, because before a player learns the various shots of the game, he must concentrate on the fundamentals of delivery and the draw shot. Until these basic skills are acquired no progress will be made.

Starting correctly

A good lead must be able to bowl to the jack consistently. All of us possess some ability to bowl to different distances when required, it just takes some longer than others to judge precisely what changes must be made between shorter and longer distances.

During the first few weeks of any season, whether it be the start of a new outdoor one in the Spring or an indoor one in September, it is advisable to practise length bowling. This is not only good for improving drawing ability, but is also of benefit in helping your concentration, especially if you can find some space on your own.

Accuracy will improve as concentration develops, and with the subsequent improvement confidence will also grow. To bowl accurately over any given period of time a player must be mentally alert, but physically relaxed. Relaxed muscles are essential to concentration; taut muscles and nerves will always let you down.

Once on the mat your concentration must be one hundred per cent until your delivery is completed. When gone, you can relax a little until your next bowl; however, always bear in mind— especially in singles play—that you need to pay some attention to the game all the time.

The competent lead must also be able to draw equally well on both hands. It is rare that you will play on a rink that has two perfect drawing hands, and the sensible lead will usually keep to the good side of the rink, which may entail bowling forehand one way and backhand the other.

Any beginner will soon realise that

it is just as important to be able to play well on other greens as at one's own club. A good lead bowler must adapt to varying conditions and must settle down quickly. This obviously applies to a bowler in any position. The ability to adapt to changing conditions, especially on outdoor greens, is essential. A good player will be able to achieve a consistently high standard of play, even when the pressure is on. It is of little merit to play brilliantly in a friendly roll-up or practice, and then to fail when the heat is on.

However, leading well is only one part of the game. A good player must be armed with every shot in the book to succeed. For example, the firing shot, despised by many players, is an essential, but a bowler must be able to revert immediately to the draw or resting shot after playing 'heavy'. It is no good firing accurately and then taking several deliveries to return to a length bowl. So, always be careful how you use the drive. If played at the wrong time, it can be very costly.

The player on the mat in a team game relies on his skip to provide precise instructions. Here Scottish skip Willie Wood makes it fairly obvious where he wants the next bowl.

Length

It is usually players with a 'good touch' who soon succeed in bowls. Being able to find a length and maintain it, whether this is achieved through a long or short delivery swing, is a skill every bowler should try to acquire.

Some bowlers will need a long backswing for the longer jack lengths, while others will obtain the same result with very little backlift. The difference will be made up by the use of gravity or direct muscle control. In the case of the longer backswing, the delivery weight of the bowl is controlled by the amount of swing, while the 'wrist' bowler will adjust his weight with muscle power.

The delivery style is often affected by the particular stance adopted. A crouch style of delivery encourages a firmer grip, with the bowl propulsion being made more from the wrist, while the athletic stance lends itself to control from the pendulum-like semi-circular backswing.

It is also important to finish your delivery correctly. At the end of the swing the palm of the hand should face upwards, with the fingers pointing along the line of delivery. This ensures that the bowl will travel along your selected line without wobbling.

It is a known fact that most badly delivered bowls are 'narrow', as opposed to too 'wide', because of incorrect footwork or turning the hand at the point of delivery. Your whole body, shoulders, knees, hips and eyes, should face the direction that the bowl must take. If the stance is not right and the hand is twisted on delivery, you will not be able to achieve accuracy or consistency.

The firmer the shot, the more accentuated the follow-through. Because of the increased weight transfer needed when the delivery velocity is greater, the delivery stride will also be longer.

Top photograph sequence on pages 38 and 39—*The style of a champion. Oxford's Irene Molyneux on her way to winning the English Ladies Indoor Singles title, with a silky smooth delivery and her unmistakable full follow-through.*

Left—*A familiar shot of David Bryant showing his characteristic high-kicking back-foot lift—all part of a smooth follow-through.*

Judgement of distance

Accurate judgement of distance to provide good length bowling is fundamental to the success of a bowler. To achieve this, the bowler must be able to estimate the amount of land required by a bowl so that it will curve with the natural bias to finish on his target, be it the jack, a bowl or simply a position in the head.

As explained in the previous chapter, the widest point over which a bowl travels before it begins to curve towards the jack is called the shoulder of the arc, and just outside that mark is the point of aim. How far from the centre-line this point will be is dependent on many factors, such as the weight of the green, the length of the jack, climatic conditions and the sort of bowl being used.

On wet and heavy greens the amount of land taken, i.e. the line over which the bowl will travel, will be less than on a dry green, and more land must be taken for a short jack than for a long one.

The general levels of a green will be important as well, and this affects both indoor and outdoor

The shoulder will alter for shots played at different paces. Here we see what the shoulder will be for the draw, the yard-on, the running shot, and the drive.

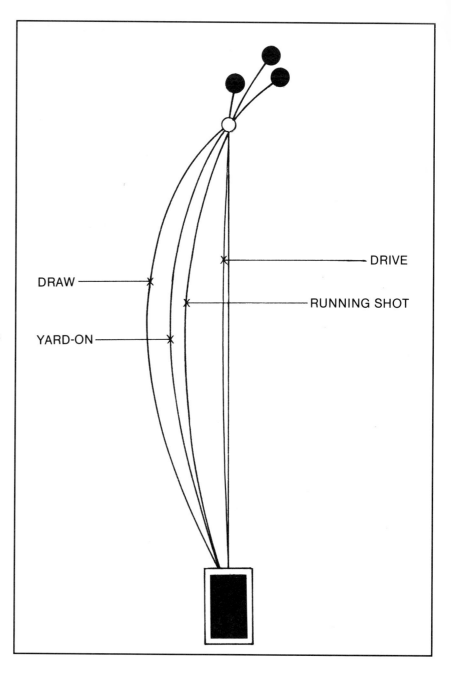

DRIVE

DRAW

RUNNING SHOT

YARD-ON

bowling, as many greens will have rinks where there is a wide drawing hand on one side and a narrow drawing hand on the other. It is important in such cases to fix your point of aim accordingly. To the experienced player, it comes quite naturally (this is when trial ends can be so important, particularly when playing on an unfamiliar green). He will quickly size up the various characteristics and drawing qualities with the first few ends and make his adjustments accordingly. However, for the beginner, it is not quite that simple.

The beginner must realise, therefore, that to draw accurately he must know his bowls' capabilities on different types of green and, if he has only one set, he must know both their advantages and limitations. His stance, delivery and follow-through will be crucial in determining the quality of his shot.

A rather unorthodox delivery but somewhat remarkable when you consider that the player on the mat is a member of a rare breed of bowler —he is totally blind! Blind bowlers use a clock system to determine line, and vocal assistance is given to determine jack length and bowl positions.

A player should be able to visualise from the mat the length of the jack and, if he has played short or through, be able to adjust accordingly. Finding and keeping a length depends on eye co-ordination and transfering the right command through the brain to the muscles.

If you find that your bowls are continually finishing short, it is a good idea to play well up and then to reduce the length; reverse the procedure if playing heavy. When playing short, mentally measure the extra length you require to reach your target, and try to remedy the problem by doubling that length when next delivering.

The famous Scottish international skip, Willie McQueen, always asks a player who is bowling short to bowl to a point a few feet behind the jack in order to get him to reach.

Checklist

The mechanics of delivering a bowl may seem fairly simple at first, but the new bowler will soon realise that they are more complex than he imagined. It often happens that the newcomer, after an initial session of being shown how to hold a bowl, how to stand and then propel his bowl up the green, finds it quite easy. He is without inhibitions and does not have the bowler's experienced 'check-list' in his mind, i.e. how much weight? how much land? etc.

It is when the novice has played in a few matches and club competitions that he begins to ask himself questions, and he may find that his game is not quite what he thought it was. Usually the faults are with the mechanics of his delivery and he will need to think about the following:

1. *Am I losing my balance?* If this is the case, the player should check that his left hand (for the right-hander) is on the left knee or thigh for steadiness and that the forward step is not too long or too short.

2. *Why is my bowl wobbling on its path up the green?* Check the grip. The middle finger should be along the centre-line surface of the bowl. Over-gripping with the

A stylish young delivery—backfoot on mat, weight transferred over front foot and arm following through.

thumb or little finger will not allow for a smooth release.

3. *Why am I bowling narrow?*
Check that your step forwards is along the line of delivery. Wrong positioning of the feet on the mat can also give a false line. Twisting of the wrist or hand at the moment of release will affect the bowl's line of travel. Check that the bowl is held upright in the hand.

4. *Why am I bowling consistently short?*
Check that your backswing is sufficient and look a little further along the aiming line. This requires a constant study of the green to ensure that you are aware of its pace and what climatic conditions (if outdoor) will affect your bowl.

5. *Am I 'bumping' my bowls?*
The person the greenkeeper loves to hate! Check that you are bending sufficiently to get close enough to the ground. If you are grounding the bowl precisely, there will be virtually no sound. If you are bumping, it will give a thud, which any greenkeeper can detect from a long way off!

6. *Why are my bowls finishing wide of the head?*
Here you will need to adjust your feet on the mat to reduce the line you have previously taken. Check that your arm is drawn back close to the side of your body.

There will be other problems to confront a bowler over the many ends played but these are most of the common ones. Some players will say that the difficulty with a bowl is that it has a peculiar shape and that it does not always perform in the way they expect it to. They will also realise that getting the correct weight to play a particular shot is much more difficult than gauging the right green. It takes a great deal of time, practice and intense concentration before you become reasonably proficient at estimating length and green.

Speed of the green
The average bowler will have many problems to sort out in his mind when he begins a match. One item he will need to determine is the 'speed of the green'. For a novice it will certainly add to the confusion when he is told that a slow green is one around 9–11 seconds, while a fast green is one from 17 to 22 seconds. The 'speed of the green' is determined by the time it takes a bowl to travel from the point of delivery on the mat to a jack at a fixed position 30 yards away. If the green is heavy (slow), the arc to the jack will be considerably less than on a fast green. Therefore, the bowl will arrive at the jack in a quicker time on a 'slow' green.

The novice bowler will soon discover that he can control his weight and pace with the length of his step and by changing the length of the backswing to give velocity to the bowl. This will help him to play the variety of shots he will soon be required to develop.

DRAW SHOTS
Drawing shots that nestle close to the jack are the ones which win matches, so try to utilise those valuable trial end bowls to learn as much as possible about land and length.

Drawing to the jack basically requires having the proper weight and choosing the correct path to the jack (land). There is little point in achieving a good rhythmic delivery if you cannot choose the correct path to the jack. To do this successfully, two problems must be faced.

The first is to decide how far out from the centre line you should deliver your bowl to compensate for its bias and to allow it to finish on the centre line. The line will soon be established in the early stages of play, although it may vary slightly depending on the distance of the jack.

On the outdoor green, of course, the weather can have a major effect on play. A heavy shower of rain can soon make conditions different: you may find that you have to take less land than before; whereas if the sun dries out a previously wet green, you may be forced to go wider.

Even the state of the green can make a difference to play. A well-cut green will tend to run faster than one poorly cut. These vagaries of outdoor greens are what make bowls both endearing and infuriating. Indoor bowls does not suffer to the same extent.

Whatever else players, coaches and anyone connected with the game argue about, there is one point you will always find them agreeing upon and that is that the *draw shot* is the most important shot in the game.

Basically, the *draw shot* is a played bowl which uses its bias to finish as close as possible to its objective, without touching another bowl on the way. The target is normally the jack, but the bowl can be played to any other spot on the green. A draw shot can be played on either hand but the mechanics of the shot are basically similar and, as explained earlier, it is a case of positioning the feet correctly on the mat, facing the aiming-line with the whole body moving rhythmically down the line and making sure that the bowl is perfectly grounded.

The draw shot is also used to gain position bowls, which may be some distance from the jack, and to beat

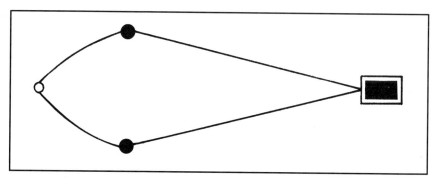

The most important shot in bowls is the draw shot. You will have to learn precisely how much your bowl will curve as it travels up the green. The amount a bowl will 'bias' is illustrated. A bowl will bias because of its shape, which is elliptical and not round.

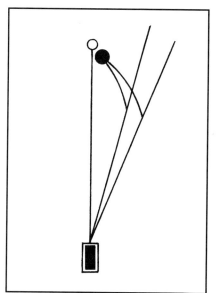

This particular shot serves two purposes: it provides a potential scoring shot and at the same time makes the hand more difficult for your opponent.

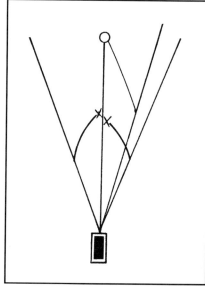

The object of playing a bowl into a 'blocking' position is to force your opponent to play a shot he does not really favour and to protect the head or a particular hand.

another bowl, in which case you may need to allow for extra green and weight: instead of taking your arc back from the jack, you may have to take it back through the position that you require your shot to finish in. Avoid playing a bowl which runs across the centre-line and finishes narrow of the jack.

The **resting shot** should be used when you are playing to reach an opponent's bowl because it may not be possible to reach the jack, or you may gain another shot from this position. It is not to be confused with a **wresting shot** which is played with enough weight to reach an opponent's bowl and to turn it over sufficiently to take its place. A better description for the latter shot would be a firm draw; it depends largely on how far you want the opponent's bowl to be turned away.

The final draw shot—the **block shot**—is one of the most difficult to play but if executed with accuracy it can be a most frustrating shot for opponents.

The object of this shot is to protect a position in the head. It is played short to force an opponent to play the shot you want him to rather than the one he was hoping to play. It is usually played to protect a good head position from an opponent's drive.

When attempting the block shot the same principles apply as for

the draw shot. The point at which the player wishes his bowl to come to rest is the target and the arc is drawn back from this point. Correct positioning of the feet is essential.

The draw shot is the most essential to any player, but success in the game will also depend on mastery of the other shots. We have looked at the draw and its variations; in the next category come the yard-on, trail, and wick.

The **yard-on shot** is one of very controlled pace and is designed to reach a target some three feet behind its objective. It is sometimes used to play out another bowl or is simply a bowl that finishes in such a position that it does not touch another bowl and will provide a cover for a possible future shot. If it fails to achieve its objective in the head, it will not be wasted if it is positioned about three feet behind.

It is a percentage bowl and is easier to play on slow or medium paced greens.

If played effectively, the **trail shot**

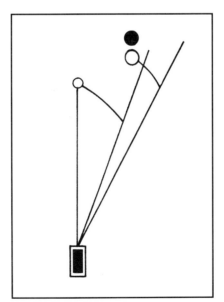

It is often necessary to play a bowl to a certain position in the head rather than to the jack. It is still, however, a draw shot—but to an imaginary jack.

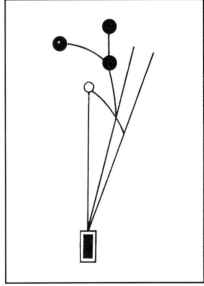

Shots can be obtained by playing out or wresting an opponent's bowl. Play with a little weight, just enough to remove the opponent's bowl and for your bowl to stay nearby in the head.

is a potential match winner. The object of this shot is to carry the jack back a specified distance and success depends very much on taking the right grass-line with the right weight. Again, the player should concentrate on the finishing position and should get the thought of the jack out of his mind. If the jack has to be taken back six feet, then that is the amount of extra pace required. When played accurately the bowl will pick up the jack on its way through, and if it misses it may still finish in a useful position. The one danger is slicing the jack, which usually happens when too much weight is applied.

The **wick shot** is often much maligned and in many cases will be dismissed as a fluke. However, a well executed wick, which uses another bowl to achieve its objective, can be extremely effective. Wick shots are normally played with a yard or two of running and their degree of turn or swing will be governed by their angle of entry into the head. The final series of shots—the run-through, the fast running shot and the drive (or fire)—are best described as the heavyweights.

The **run-through shot** is a bowl played with enough pace to upset the head. It is played to disturb short bowls which will then run through to a good back position. Several extra yards of pace will

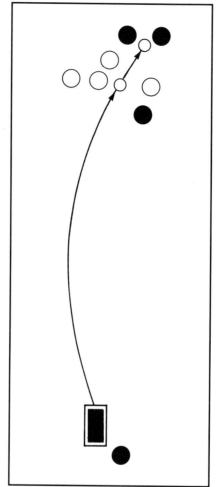 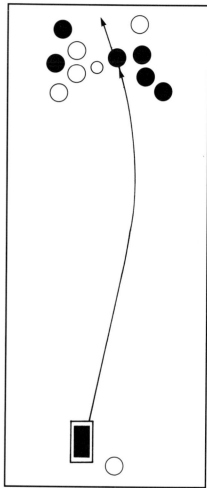

Match situations. Here is an example of a trail shot situation. The black bowl player has the last bowl, but is three down to white. If he can play with just enough weight to move the jack a yard through the head to his two back bowls, he could count three himself.

White has the last bowl and is just one shot down, although it is close. However, if he can remove the black bowl he could lie three shots. Here he must play with more weight and take less green to achieve his objective. The take-out bowl may not stay in the count but it would be two shots, which is a conversion of three.

be required, with the necessary cutting down of the grass-line—depending largely on the pace of the green. A faster running shot is the **heavy bowl** which is similar but is played with ditch weight and should it miss its objective it will come to rest in the ditch. The shot is invaluable when you are required to move a single bowl from the head or take the jack into the ditch.

THE SHOTS

1. A well played wick shot can be very effective. Bowlers tend to look on it as a fluke but, as the illustration shows, playing with just enough weight to divert off the side bowl will give you the shot.

2. With the trail shot you need to move the jack either to give you the advantage or to save a bad situation (in many cases it is both!). The grassline will depend on how far you want the jack to travel—the longer the trail, the narrower the grassline.

3. With a running shot you need to play with enough weight to move a bowl through the head while hoping to stay in the head to gain the shot yourself. The effect of hitting another bowl stuns the path of your own bowl. The grassline is adjusted according to the pace required.

4. Here are two examples of the grassline required for a drive. The shot is often delivered with enough force to counteract the natural bias of a bowl. You will have to study the green to know what is your required grassline.

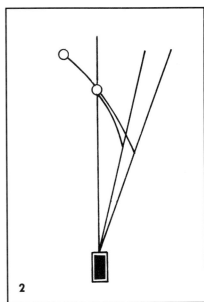

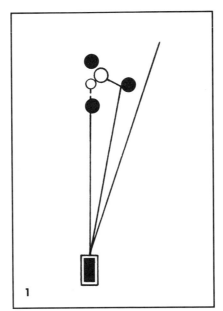

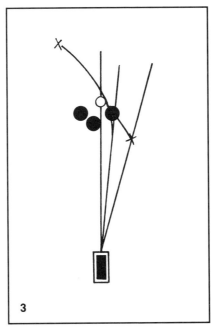

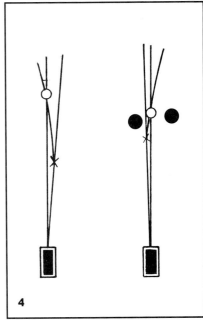

A bowl played at maximum controlled pace is called the **drive**. Its objective will be to remove a bowl, open up the head, kill the head, or take the jack into the ditch. It is a shot that causes a lot of ill-feeling in the sport of bowls, mainly because it can destroy a carefully planned head with just one blow. Many critics contend that driving spoils the game, but they are generally those players who can't use the shot accurately enough themselves.

The drive is the power shot of bowls and requires excellent balance and follow-through. Any jerk in the delivery is to be avoided. It can wreak havoc and you should always pose the following questions before undertaking it: what do I stand to gain?, what do I stand to lose?, what are the chances of success or will it go against me?

When driving, a player should play the shot on the hand which ensures that the bias of the bowl will take it towards the bowls that he wants to hit. And remember, you must not sacrifice direction for speed.

The crowd buzzes as David Bryant strikes the pose for the firing shot that can instil instant apprehension in opponents. Here David stands square on the mat, looking straight down the rink with his bowl gripped tight. Transfer of bodyweight will be well forward.

In all cases, the foundation for each shot is the right amount of weight (or pace).

The jack

It is as well to remember at this stage that because most shots in bowls are directed at the jack it is most important to be able to bowl the jack to the lengths required, whether leading or playing in singles competitions. Many skips can lose the art of casting the jack if they do not play in singles and always play in backend positions.

The jack is not biased and will therefore roll in a straight line. If the jack deviates from a straight line, it will provide useful information about the surface condition of the green. Having centred the mat correctly, the jack should be rolled easily out of the hand, using a similar technique to that of delivering a bowl. Your feet should be pointing in the direction of the line you wish to take, which in this case is in a straight line forwards from the mat.

The minimum cast of the jack is 25 yards from the front edge of the mat and the maximum cast is to within 6 feet of the edge of the green. If any part of the jack comes to rest over the dividing string, it is considered 'dead'. When the jack comes to rest it is centred in a direct line with the rink centre-pins.

In the case of a player who delivers the jack too short or off the green, the jack is returned and re-delivered by the other player, although the original player still bowls first. If both players fail to set the jack twice, the jack is then placed 6 feet from the front edge of the ditch to a mat length determined by the first player.

A good lead should be able to place the jack at whatever length he or his skip directs. He should also work hard to play his shots equally well on both hands.

The novice bowler should remember that bowls is a game in which you never stop learning and that to improve you must have some, perhaps most, of the following qualities: the ambition to achieve your aims; enthusiasm and love for the game; courage and endurance (despite its appearance, bowls is a sport that needs a certain amount of stamina and fitness); a good mind to work out the best shots to play and then to execute them; and a certain ruthlessness and determination to succeed.

Always remember that the objective of building a head is to prevent the opposition from getting

Deliver the jack from the tips of the fingers, as there is less tendency for it to go off line, making sure your feet point down the delivery line.

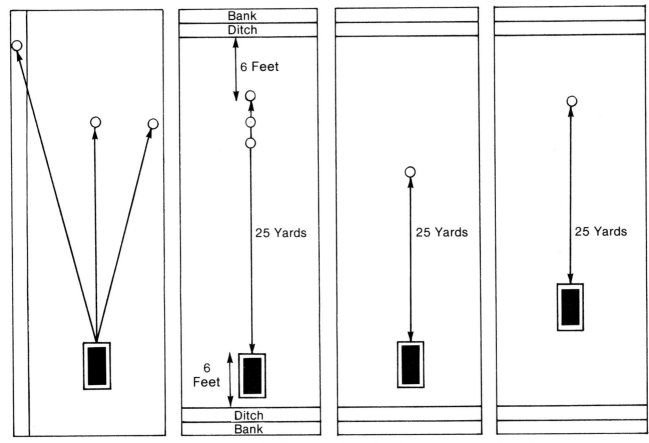

DELIVERING THE JACK

Delivering the jack. *Always try to deliver the jack down the centre line of the rink. Haphazard delivery can lead to the jack going off the rink, which then gives your opponent a chance to set his length.*

On the first end the front edge of the mat must be 6 feet from the ditch and the jack must be not less than 25 yards (22.8 metres) from the front edge of the mat and a minimum of 6 feet from the front edge of the back ditch.

Good use of the mat and jack can help you win a match. You can keep the mat back and play a short-length jack or take the mat up the green and play a short-length jack that way. Some players like to vary the mat and jack lengths constantly during opening ends; others will keep to a length they are finding successful.

the shot or, if they do, to be able to convert the position to a favourable one. Take care at all times to give the game your full attention and observe the basic principles of bowling.

The mat

It is also important to use your mat correctly. Stand on the mat (which measures 24" × 14") to deliver your bowl. The rules dictate that for the start of play the mat must be laid on the centre-line of the rink, with its front edge not less than 6 feet from the rear ditch. After that, providing that the jack is 25 yards from the front edge and no less than 6 feet from the front of the ditch, you can move the mat up and down the green.

The mat may seem a very simple piece of equipment but it can be made to work for you. You can make use of the mat to alter the position along the centre of the green to avoid any peculiarities, to alter your feet positions in order to play a narrow or wider bowl or to secure an advantage over an opponent.

If you feel that an opponent is playing well to a certain length, you may, on winning an end, move the mat to try to put him off his length. Combined use of mat and jack length are often useful tactical ploys in altering the nature of a game.

4 TACTICS AND STRATEGY

A successful team is a unit in which all players combine harmoniously and thoroughly enjoy the exercise. To achieve this team members must appreciate the psychology of the game and must think positively at all times.

There are some very obvious differences between playing singles and the team games of pairs, triples and fours. In singles the player is bowling for fifty per cent of the time. The percentage decreases as the number of players increases; for example, in fours you share the mat with seven other people and so are only bowling for around $12\frac{1}{2}\%$ of the time! It is, nevertheless, still important to maintain your concentration in the non-bowling moments as well as during the periods when you are on the mat.

It is especially difficult for the leads and no. 2s, because after they have bowled their duties have finished until the conclusion of that particular end. However, the no. 2 in a rinks game is also responsible for keeping the score (both card and scoreboard). The no. 3s still have a specific task to perform after they have bowled and will be the skip's right-hand players while the leads and no. 2s are bowling.

In most cases a lead will spend about a minute of an average six- or seven-minute end actually bowling. However, he still needs to be involved as part of the team. He can do this by adopting a positive attitude towards encouraging his team-mates. In team play there is often too much time spent standing around saying nothing: it is far better to acknowledge your team-mates' good bowls and to make your presence felt, as this will help to boost the confidence of the whole team.

Anyone who has ever seen the former Scottish international skip, Harry Reston, will know that one man's enthusiasm, his friendly and genuine pleasure in his fellow bowlers' success, can boost overall morale sky-high—natural

enthusiasm can be worth many shots in the closing stages of a match.

Unfortunately, such interest is far from common in everyday club bowls, but there really is a tremendous amount of pleasure to be gained by becoming completely absorbed in a match, much more than just standing around idly chatting until it is your turn to bowl again.

There is also nothing unsporting in keenness and eagerness providing they are genuine and spontaneous. Sometimes the over-enthusiasm one sees on a bowls green springs from a desire to cry down opponents as much as to lift an individual team.

Scoring

There are four types of game in flat green bowls—singles, pairs, triples and fours.

In singles matches each player usually plays four bowls, although there are many two-bowl competitions, particularly in

Federation competitions. The games comprise 21-up shots, although there are variations to this: sometimes a lower number of shots or a time-limit is introduced, and some clubs also have handicap competitions in which one player may be given a certain number of shots to start with.

The pairs game is played with four bowls per player up to 21 ends. As in rinks a tied end is an end played, but a dead end has to be replayed. Should the scores be level after 21 ends, extra ends are played until a result is obtained.

With three bowls per player the triples game can be a lengthy affair, although it is usually played over 18 ends and not 21. In Federation bowling two bowls per player forms the basis of the game, but a three-bowl triples is included in the national competitions.

In fours (or rinks) each player has two bowls and the game is played over 21 ends. The lead (or first man) places the mat and casts the jack, the no. 2 keeps the score, the no. 3 (or third) is second in command and measures shots, while the skip is in control of the team.

Mixed pairs and fours bowling are becoming more popular, with the new national competitions launched by both indoor and outdoor authorities receiving record entries. It has often been said that the sole

object of bowls is to get your bowls nearer to the jack than your opponent's—and that makes for an easy scoring system. You count however many of your bowls are closer to the jack than your opponent's nearest bowls to determine the score on any particular end.

Each bowl that finishes nearer the jack than your opponent's best bowl scores one point. The score is recorded after each player (or group of players) has delivered all his bowls from one end of the green to the jack at the other. After that play then takes place in the reverse direction.

A new type of scoring system—the 'sets scoring' system—has now been introduced through the medium of television. It has mainly been used for singles; players play up to a set number (in most cases seven-up) for the 'best of' a number of sets (usually three). In the case of major championships which appear on television the first round is over three sets, the following rounds over five and the final over nine. The Liverpool Victoria Superbowl event, which mixes 16 top crown players with 16 top flat green players, keeps to three sets throughout.

DUTIES

Accepting the necessity for everyone to maintain concentration and to encourage all other members of the team to bowl as well as they can, what are the specific duties of each player in a fours team?

The first duty of a lead lies in placing the mat. On the first end he must do this in accordance with the laws of the game, which dictate that there should be 6 feet from the front edge of the mat to the front edge of the ditch. After that the mat can be placed in any position up the green from this point, providing that the jack is a minimum of 25 yards from its front edge.

The lead is required to put two bowls right in the head, which can be used for promoting, resting or running through, and which are delivered from a mat position chosen by the skip. Here the lead must accept his skip's desire for a certain mat length, and should consider his team as a unit and should not concentrate on the length at which he is best. Mat positioning can play an important part in team tactics, as can the placing of the jack.

In many ways the no. 2 is complementary to the lead and as such his task may be to achieve what the lead has failed to do, or he may simply have to block or improve a promising position. The no. 2 is often not highly rated—wrongly so—it is actually a very important part of any fours team. He must be just as strong as the remainder of the team and must even possess extra qualities, particularly that of patience. This is required because a no. 2 often has to bowl to 'blank' positions rather than to a clearly visible target. If the shot is against him, the no. 2 is normally asked to play a specific shot: if not, he must put two useful bowls into the head, making sure that he has sized up the swing of the green.

It is also the duty of the no. 2 to keep the scorecard. He should check continually throughout the game with his opposite number that it is correct. At the end of the game the scorecard should be handed to the skip.

A no. 3 who can play a fast bowl and one who could play all the game's shots if need be is a good choice. Obviously a competent all-rounder is ideal, but one must bear in mind that at club level it is often difficult to find the complete player.

If the lead and no. 2 are reasonable length bowlers, then they should be able to get somewhere near the jack; it is always an easier task for a no. 3 to have some kind of target or resting place at which to aim. A no. 3 will offer advice to his skip, but only when it is necessary, for example, if the position has altered after the skip left the head, or the no. 3 feels that another inspection of the head is called for. However, nothing can be more infuriating for a skip than to be on the mat preparing to bowl and then to be interrupted suddenly by the no. 3 dancing around and shouting fresh advice.

At the completion of an end the no. 3s will agree the score. The right to measure is also in the hands of the no. 3s. Any disagreements can be settled by the skips.

The skip of the rink must watch every move on the board. He will have to weigh up the strengths and weaknesses of the opposition and extract every ounce of skill out of his own team. The skip must discover the best way of motivating each person. One player may need encouragement, another flattery, while another might be a little impetuous and need to be curbed. The skip is in sole charge of the rink and while listening to the opinions of his colleagues he must have a definite shot in mind when he steps on the mat—still to be in two minds at such a stage can be fatal. At the start of each game a skip will introduce his players to their opposite numbers.

On the playing side, the skip must be capable of making all shots and should have a great deal of experience. It is not sufficient just to be a consistent bowler; a skip must have the knowledge of building a head and managing a rink. There will always be two types of skip—the adventurous and the cautious. Choose the style best suited to your skills and give it a good trial.

Always bear in mind that bowls should be a pleasurable game and, on the whole, being over-cautious can spoil that pleasure.

Team members' responsibilities

We have dealt with the individuals in the rink, so what are the points to remember for making a good team member?

1. Be a player everyone enjoys having on the rink.

2. Only praise—never criticise. When a player is on the mat about to deliver his bowl he should feel that he has the backing of every member of the team. This applies particularly to the skip who always has to play more pressure bowls than any other team member.

3. A good skip discusses tactics with his team, as it is necessary that they should feel their contributions are an important part of the game. However, he has to make the final decisions and he cannot please everybody, so whatever he decides he must know he has the confidence of his fellow team-mates.

4. Be a confidence booster. If you are a skip, never forget that however off-form a member of the rink may be, no player ever deliberately steps on to the mat to deliver a bad bowl. Always try to help by discussing the playing conditions, by introducing a little humour to relieve the tensions, by thinking deeply about the players' problems and, therefore, by devising a tactical solution.

5. Do not be a selfish player. Always consider what is best for

Opposite—A skip should give the members of his team clear instructions about where he wants a bowl played.

55

the team. What you like personally may not be best for the unit. This applies particularly to the lead with the placing of the mat and jack.

6. Listen to all instructions carefully and be quite clear about what is required of you. Endeavour to comply with your skip's requests, giving full concentration and effort when delivering the bowl, and shutting out all other distractions even if the shot you are playing is not of your own personal choice.

7. A good skip is one who is amenable, approachable, has a sense of humour, always appears relaxed, encourages his team and helps players. No member of a four should ever have to think twice about discussing tactics with his skip, and if his suggestion is not accepted he must realise that it was only discarded after careful consideration. He must then obey the decision and should not let it affect his game.

Skips convey messages by hand movements and vocal instructions. A no. 2 can be seen checking the score.

8. Harmony is the key to success: this can be achieved by open discussion off the rink.

9. Be conversant with the laws of the game.

5 MATCH PREPARATION

Having covered the basic art of delivering a bowl, the moment will soon come when you have to put this to use in a match. You will probably be apprehensive, nervous or tense, so perhaps the first thing to learn is to relax a little. However, the most important factor is to get your concentration right. You should begin concentrating the moment the coin is tossed, whether you are involved in a singles or a team event.

If you are in a team event it will be in your interest to play as lead so that you can begin to master the basic art of bowls, which is drawing to the jack. Numerous players make the mistake of putting a new player at no. 2 in a rink. Many top players will tell you that, far from being a weak position where you can 'hide' a

One of the many top young players in the game, John Leeman of Stanley in Durham, seen here on his way to victory in the final of the Lombard Champion of Champions.

beginner, the no. 2 slot is the most crucial position in any rink.

When playing, particularly at lead, you have the choice of taking either the forehand or backhand shot. Assuming that your opponent has played the green before, he will probably take his favourite hand. He will know roughly how the particular rink plays, but in the trial ends you will get a look at the green as well—so watch your opponent's bowls as well as your own. In most matches you are allowed two 'trial' ends which will give you a practice feel of the green. Use these wisely to get an idea of the pace of the green and of the state of the two 'hands'.

Try to make your delivery as smooth as possible, ensure you are gripping your bowl correctly (a wobbling bowl cannot be consistently accurate), and check to see that your stance on the mat is right.

USE OF THE MAT

1. Feet in normal position for a straightforward draw shot.

2. Feet moved to one side of the mat to play around the bowl which appears in the eye. The track is slightly more than that of a normal draw, and the bowl is played with a little more weight.

3. Here the shot is played slightly inside the bowl that appears in the eye, and with less weight.

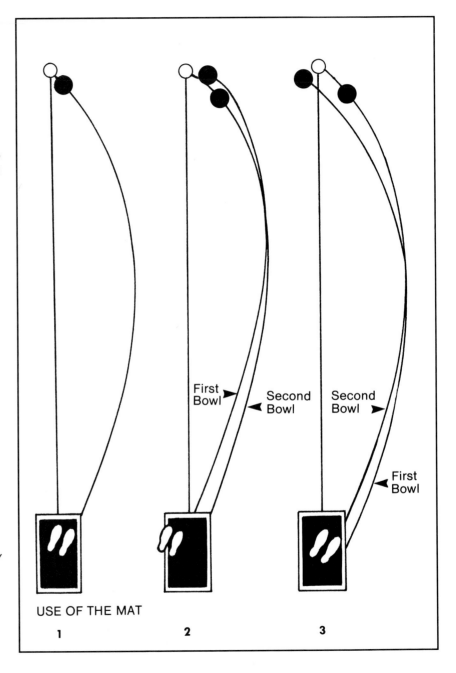

First Bowl

Second Bowl

Second Bowl

First Bowl

USE OF THE MAT

1   2   3

As with many aspects of bowls, your position on the mat is a matter of personal preference. There is only one rule that you must follow: at the moment the bowl touches the playing surface, at least one foot must be on or directly above the mat. To help develop a controlled, comfortable and rhythmic delivery, many people suggest that you stand in the centre of the mat, with both feet comfortably positioned a few inches apart, making sure that they are parallel with each other. If your feet are correctly positioned, your whole body should be facing along the line of delivery.

Australian Ken Williams illustrates the perfect athletic delivery. Body is nicely relaxed and knees are slightly bent, with four fingers in an orthodox position below the bowl and thumb to the side, and feet pointing along the delivery line.

Correct line

The theory behind finding your correct green line is simple. The line is governed by the angle which it forms with the centre line somewhere on the mat. Each bowl in a set is manufactured with an identical bias, and each bowl will therefore draw or curve to precisely the same extent. Once you have found this correct line it is just a question of keeping to it. Although it is difficult to master, finding the correct land is vital if you hope to progress in the game.

How does the beginner go about finding the correct land? It does help to try to find a starting point: choose a spot on the bank, to the right of the centre-marker,

The bowling hand and arm are now starting the backswing. Feet are still pointing along the delivery line and the head is motionless. The arm brushes past the slightly bent right knee.

assuming you are a right-handed bowler about to play a forehand shot. Line up your centre-line, then adjust your feet to point along the new green line. Some bowlers prefer to use the green and the jack to measure that imaginary line, which helps to develop judgement and self-confidence.

Beginners are generally inclined to bowl straight for the jack. It is possibly a nervous reaction to seeing a bowl going away from its target at first. They do not take enough 'green'. You may see your bowl cutting across the head and finishing on the other side of the jack, or perhaps it stops short of the centre line, failing to reach by about six feet. If this happens, you must adjust your angle. Re-position your feet and take either a wider line, if you are bowling narrow, or cut down on the amount of green you have been taking if you have been finishing too wide. Constant practice is the only way you will be able to master the art of finding the right green.

From end to end, and often actually during an end, the distance between the mat and jack will vary. Also, you may be required to play to a spot that is some distance from the jack. It is therefore important to be able to control the length of your delivery.

When the bowl leaves your hand it begins to travel in a straight line

The movement of the backswing coincides with the forward step of the left leg, which also provides for balanced co-ordination of the transfer of bodyweight.

The distance which the left leg goes forwards should roughly correspond with the bowler's length to obtain the correct amount of bodyweight transfer. The left hand is coming on to the knee to assist further with body balance.

under the force that you apply to it. As the bowl loses its momentum, the bias begins to affect its course and it curves inwards towards its target. This point at which the bowl begins to curve is called the 'shoulder' of the green. A fact which can be helpful is that the shoulder is usually level with a point about two-thirds of the distance between the front of the mat and the point at which the bowl finally comes to rest. Once you have acquired some measure of confidence in bowling along a predetermined line, you should then concentrate on bowling at the shoulder.

You should aim to deliver your bowl with just enough force to reach the shoulder so that the bias will then take over and draw the bowl to the jack. Extra pace can be gained by taking a slightly longer step forwards when delivering. This will naturally increase the length of your back swing. The elbow of your delivery arm should be comfortably at your side, with the forearm almost parallel to the ground.

Length

Most bowlers will agree it is better to err on the side of heaviness when having difficulty in finding or maintaining a consistent length. There are two main reasons for this: the first is that back bowls are always in the head as the jack is often trailed back, and the second is that it is easier to decrease length accurately than to increase it. If you find that you are bowling on the heavy side you can lessen the pace of your bowl by shortening your step forwards or by inclining your forearm downwards during delivery. In the case of a crouch-type delivery it is just a case of adjusting the length of the swing.

It will take a good deal of time, practice and intense concentration before you become reasonably proficient in estimating length and land. You can help yourself in practice by placing a disc on the point on the green at which your bowl should begin to bias towards the jack, or four or five yards in front of the mat, and by constantly bowling over this mark. Note where your bowl finishes each time.

A player who can draw well to the jack will always stand a good chance of winning games single-handed and will be an asset to any team. Some skips like to tell their lead where to place the jack, others will leave it to the lead to determine the length. If a lead is consistently drawing well to a particular length a skip will be quite happy to let him continue. If

An excellent release: back foot resting on the mat, bowl grounded perfectly from finger-tip control, and the whole of the body pointing down the delivery line. A nicely relaxed action and smooth follow-through.

things are not going well the skip might decide, when his team gets possession of the jack, to vary the length. In this case he may ask for his lead to drop a short jack, in the hope that it will upset the opposition's rhythm.

Possession of the jack is quite an important factor because it means that your team is dictating the length. In drawing to the jack try to achieve one of two aims: get your bowl either a few inches behind the jack or a few inches in front. Remember that a jack high bowl is a target and can be so easily used by your opponent.

A jack must be delivered a minimum of 25 yards (22.86 metres) from the front edge of the mat. If this distance is not reached the jack is returned and the opposing player has the choice of placing the mat and re-delivering the jack, although he does not play first.

The jack must also be placed so that the front of it is 6 feet (1.84 metres) from the front ditch, if the jack in its original course has come to rest less than 2 yards from the opposite ditch.

New laws recently introduced allow players two 'mis-casts' each. After the fourth 'mis-cast', the player who delivered the jack first will have the choice of mat placement, but the jack will be placed with its front edge 6 feet from the front ditch.

An end will be made 'dead' when the jack is driven by a bowl in play wholly beyond the boundary of the rink (i.e. over the bank or side boundary). All such 'dead' ends are played again in the same direction, unless both skips agree to play them in the opposite direction.

STUDY OF THE GREEN

It is important to have a knowledge of playing surfaces and to be able to assess how to tackle them. Cumberland turf greens were always considered the ultimate in grass bowling surfaces. They have a very fine, rounded-blade grass which is ideal for bowling. Also, because the grass is sea-washed it thrives on sand, which is a marvellous surface to play bowls on since it stays level and has fast-drying qualities, draining well. The surface can be rolled, too, and because it is on sand it does not compact. However, the grass is not very deep-rooted and so it cannot withstand droughts. This means that it has to have regular watering.

The quality of greens is always allied to greenkeeping. In the past specialist knowledge was handed down from father to son. Emphasis was placed on preparing a playing surface and a free-running green on which the player could display all his skills and attempt a full range of shots. Unfortunately, today the emphasis has changed

and is now placed on retaining healthy turf at the expense of the playing surface, which is little better than a superb lawn. The true comparison is with that of a cricketer batting on a good wicket, which is hard and true, who then has to face a bowler on a bumpy green where the ball could go anywhere. The requirements of a good cricket wicket are similar to those of a bowling green, although not to the same extent. In both cases it is essential that they be free of bumps and have a smooth, firm, evenly covered surface. The degree of compaction that takes place on a cricket wicket cannot apply to a bowling green, but a certain amount of rolling is necessary to achieve a good playing surface.

One of the problems which faced Cumberland turf was that when taken out of its natural environment other grasses tended to seed into it, thereby producing a green with a number of undesirable grass varieties. These were free-running greens, but today the trend is to use a mixture of sand and soil; peat as a top dressing has tended to slow down green speeds. The use of grass mixtures of a coarser nature also gives greater friction to the green and makes it heavier. The main reason these days, however, for heavier greens is that they are not cut as regularly or as closely as they should be. It makes a green moist because it does not dry out properly. Perhaps greens are not rolled enough either, and this, allied to the longer length of the grass, makes them slower. The more grass you leave on a green, the more you will get 'tracking'.

When he walks onto a green it is useful for a bowler to notice its characteristics so that he can assess the type of game he is going to have to play. He can then adapt himself properly to the conditions. He must remember that the pace of the green is not only determined by the closeness of the cut, or by rolling, but by how clean the grass is. If grass is not looked after there is a build up of thatch, and the less

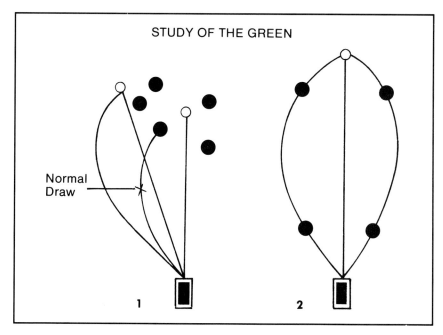

STUDY OF THE GREEN

Normal Draw

1

2

Above—*John Roberts of Littlehampton demonstrates some of the skills involved with the laying of a new green.*

STUDY OF THE GREEN (left)

1. In this head the jack has been moved well out towards the string. When trying to draw to a jack near the strings, always allow a little extra length and slightly less green to compensate for the slower surface. This applies much more on outdoor surfaces than on indoor ones.

2. You cannot always judge the length by just looking at the jack in a straight line. A study of your green will reveal whether or not a particular rink will need a wide or a narrow draw. There can be large variations in the amount of green required, depending on green speed.

it is cut down, the more thatch there will be. This gives a spongy, ripple effect which can throw a bowl off course and give peculiar runs in the green.

So, when a bowler visits a club he can usually determine how the green is going to play by examining the texture of the grass and by looking to see if the surface is polished or bumpy. It follows that it is more difficult for a player who is used to a very good green to play on a quite bad one, than the other way round. The player who bowls on a bad green has to concentrate so much on getting his line right, because he knows that if he is a fraction out he is going to go off at a tangent, whereas on a good green he will find it that much easier to get a line.

Bad greens are also usually heavier; on a nice, easy paced, reliable green, however, you can play excellent bowls. If you play on a heavy, bumpy green you have to forget about the finer arts, make up your mind right from the start that there is nothing for short-ones, make sure you get more bowls in the head than your opponent and tend to play attacking bowls. A bad green brings everyone to the same level.

The problems provided by the weather do not directly affect play on indoor synthetic surfaces. You certainly don't experience the effects of wind and rain indoors where the atmosphere is much cosier. That does not mean to say that indoor surfaces are not in some way affected by the external weather. On a cold day it will take the heaters longer to warm your stadium up and that often means the carpet will be slower. On a humid day moisture may creep into the surface and this again may affect the bowls' running.

The most important part of an indoor surface is the underlay, because this determines the pace, and performance, of each bowl. It is therefore important that the right type of carpet and underlay is chosen and that the screeding is correct.

The basic principles of the game are the same for both indoor and outdoor bowls; the main differences are atmospheric and playing conditions.

SPEED OF THE GREEN

Much will be spoken among the more experienced players about the 'speed' of the green, and this can be very confusing to the beginner. When a player talks about a 'fast' green he really means that a bowl will take longer to reach the jack than on a 'slow' green. A fast green is one where the grass is closely cut and the ground firm and dry. On a surface like this the bowl will meet little resistance as it travels to the jack and it will draw to a greater extent when the bias begins to take effect. Therefore, you will need to take a wider arc to the jack, using more land, so your bowl takes longer to reach its target.

A slow or holding green is usually soft and wet. The grass is a shade on the long side and perhaps it has been raining before you are about to play. These conditions will all help to slow down the pace of the green. You will take a much smaller arc in bowling to the jack and so your bowl will reach its target much sooner. A common fault is to underestimate the speed of a slow green, which means your bowls may consistently fall short of the jack or of your target.

It is important during play to keep a constant watch for any change in the conditions that might affect the speed of the green. A sudden shower of rain will slow the green whereas sunshine can speed it up— although you will find that if the sun shines after a shower of rain this will have the effect of slowing the green down, because the moisture is drawn to the surface; as the moisture evaporates, so the green will speed up.

Wind can also affect both the speed of the green and the amount of draw on your bowls. A steady breeze can dry out a damp surface. A strong head wind can

slow down the inward draw of your bowl, but a following wind can accentuate it. A wind blowing across the green can increase or decrease the amount of draw, depending on its direction.

Be aware of the pace of the green and the general conditions, because your arm and leg movements will be governed by them.

Finding the correct line to the jack is essential and this can be altered by a variety of conditions, particularly the weather. Shadows on the green (a) will tend to make the running slower, while the wind can alter both the speed and the amount of draw that you will need. A headwind will slow the bowl, but a following wind will speed it up. Crosswinds (b) are the most difficult to deal with, as they mean you have to increase or decrease the line to the jack, depending on direction. On sunny days (c) the green tends to be faster, thus requiring a wider draw to the jack, while rain and damp conditions (d) have the opposite effect.

6 TRAINING, PRACTICE AND TEMPERAMENT

The present generation of bowlers can thank those pioneers who not only formulated the current rules but who also were largely responsible for the introduction of the many 'unwritten laws' which are still regarded today as the etiquette of the game.

Friendships made on the bowling green are sincere and enduring, which is what gives the game its special charm. Proceedings are usually commenced with a friendly handshake and introductions all-round on first-name terms—a familiarity which creates an atmosphere of warmth and cordiality. It also creates one of sociability, which provides a pattern for acts of courtesy between team-mates, opponents, officials and spectators. The code ensures that a new club member will feel at home at once. It means, too, that no one bowler has an unfair advantage over another, because on the green all players are regarded as equal.

A pleasing gesture at the start of any game is to hand the jack to

Even a wheelchair need not be a handicap for bowling as demonstrated here by John Greenhow of the Great Britain team.

your opponent if he takes the mat first. It is also a sporting gesture to commend a good bowl of your opponent and of a player in your own team. You should find that this immediate act of friendship will be reciprocated and should create a good atmosphere for the match. It is also etiquette to acknowledge a fluke or a good rub, bearing in mind that all players bowl them at some time or other during their bowling lives.

POSITION ON THE GREEN

Sometimes players, quite unconsciously, follow their bowls up the green in such a manner as to obliterate the view of the running from their opponents. Although this is not a breach of the rules, it is quite easy to step to one side to allow an opponent sight of your bowl's path up the green. Players should also remember that when their bowl has stopped running— time being allowed for the marking of 'touchers'—they should then give possession of the rink to their

That's the shot! Arms raised in triumph, these players appreciate a good shot when it's played.

opponents should retire to a position behind the mat or the head.

You should never stand in any position that is likely to distract your opponent, or do anything that will put him off while he is about to bowl. A player should keep on his own rink and should not wander off to chat to players or people on the bank—it could be distracting to other bowlers. Always pay attention to the end being played. Nothing will be more frustrating to other members of the team than to feel that you are not giving your best because you are not concentrating fully.

Avoid wasting time arguing which is 'shot'. If there is any doubt, the person asking for the shot should get down and measure: 'if in doubt, measure out' is a guiding principle. If you still cannot agree and an umpire is called for, keep well back. Let him attend to the matter in hand and do not try to tell him how it should be done.

When a skip decides to play a 'firing' shot it is not only common sense, but a good idea, to move well out of the line of fire, even to the point of standing on the bank. This way players avoid being struck by the jack or any bowls that move quickly out of the head.

SKIPS' RESPONSIBILITIES

The skip of a rink bears special responsibility. He should never hold any player open to ridicule by shouting what is often blatantly obvious to a player. 'You're short!' or 'You're narrow!' said in a sarcastic manner can only cause friction. Informing a player that he 'needs to put a yard more on' his next bowl, in a quiet, efficient manner, is constructive and reassuring. Players know when they have bowled badly—they do not need reminding.

Constant encouragement is the keynote of success, and always giving full recognition for the good shots. One of the worst crimes that any skip can commit is to miss a good shot played by one of his team because he was chatting to his opposing skip or with spectators on the bank. The worst crime of all is for a skip to turn his back on a team member who has just delivered a bad bowl.

Skips should also avoid showing an experienced player what green to take. With novices it is obviously necessary, but the more experienced players will consider it something of an insult if a skip stands in a position and says 'use my feet as your line'. Having made this remark, however, the skip is in control of the rink at all times and if he cannot control, he should not skip—without being a despot.

Any skip worth his position should use his team to full advantage. If a

player cannot quite see the shot that he is being asked to play, the skip should keep advising him of its necessity, even asking him to come up to the head and inspect.

Finally, always try to be on time for a game or, if unexpectedly delayed, do attempt to get a message to your opponent—it will be appreciated.

To sum up the points on etiquette:

1. Always dress correctly for all games.

2. Compliment your opponent on a good bowl.

3. Stand still when a player is about to bowl. Do not talk or make a noise behind the mat when a player is delivering.

4. Remain behind the mat or behind the head when it is not your turn to play. As soon as your bowl comes to rest, possession of the rink passes to your opponents. Keep to your own rink. Do not become a wanderer and distract other bowlers.

5. On a bright, sunny day be aware of your shadow. Do not let it mask the jack, or permit it to fall in front of the mat when your opponent is about to deliver. Try to avoid obscuring boundary pegs, rink plates and markers.

6. Never criticise, only praise.

7. Pay attention to the game. Nothing can be more frustrating to your partners than to feel that you are not giving your best through lack of concentration. Always appear to enjoy the game, whatever the fortunes.

8. Stand well back from the head when firing shots are played. If a jack or bowl makes contact with a player, ensure that it is not you! Many unfortunate incidents could be avoided with a little common sense.

Opposite—*Whatever the result, the ability to win or lose gracefully is an important part of good bowls etiquette. Here Scotland's Bob Sutherland congratulates his losing final opponent, Burnie Gill of Canada, in a World Indoor Singles at Coatbridge IBC (Glasgow).*

7 FAULT-FINDING AND CORRECTION

As a check-list of bowling principles the following set of 'Dos and Don'ts' is a must for all aspiring bowlers and for the more experienced who may have forgotten them.

DO'S

1. Be conversant with the laws of the game.

2. Make sure that you are gripping your bowl correctly. A wobbling bowl will not be consistently accurate.

3. Check to ensure that when you adopt your stance on the mat you are facing the shoulder of the arc of the hand you wish to play. Remember to be perfectly balanced and relaxed, with knees slightly bent if bowling in the athletic position.

4. Make sure that your whole body flows through your delivery, from the hand which delivers the bowl to the back foot that lifts gently off the mat.

5. Be very aware of the pace and general conditions of the green, because your arm and leg movements will be governed by them. The faster the green, the more alive the bowl will become

A study in pre-delivery concentration from Jeanette Conlan, a former British Isles and Scottish Ladies Indoor Singles Champion.

and the more sensitive the touch required. On heavier greens the bowl should be caressed by the fingers and the whole mechanics of the delivery made more delicate; the movement will be slower and the backswing shorter, and with a long, graceful follow-through the delivery becomes a gliding motion.

6. Having estimated weight by looking at the jack, keep your eyes firmly fixed on the shoulder of the intended arc when delivering the bowl and keep your head down until after the bowl has been released.

7. Practise, practise, practise, and try to become proficient in all the shots of the game. Remember that there is a perfect weight and green combination for every shot attempted and nothing gives more satisfaction than to apply it successfully. Mastery of this combination is the hardest part of the game, but the ability to play shots with correct weight and green is a great asset.

8. Always be positive when you step on the mat. Be sure of the shot

that you wish to play, and always stand well back from the mat when your opponent is in play. Never be too eager to play your bowl: take your time and fully assess the position before you bowl. Remember to use the mat and jack intelligently. Have a sound reason for every tactical move you make.

9. When you are playing in pairs, triples or fours and you are not skipping, always remember that it is a team game. There is only one man in command so mould your play to his wishes. Four players, no matter how good, playing their own games will never make a successful rink.

10. In singles play you cannot afford to waste any bowl and these games are therefore the ones in which it is easiest for a bowler to build up or improve self-discipline and deep concentration.

11. When playing lead or no. 2 in a four, encourage your third man and skip, but do not let your enthusiasm get out of hand to the extent that it becomes a nuisance. Remember that the third and skip are in control and other players should keep well back where they can take an interest without interfering and confusing the issue.

12. Watch your opponent's game carefully and look for weaknesses which you may be able to exploit profitably at a suitable time in the match.

Bill Moseley of South Africa keeping a keen eye on the path of David Bryant's bowl during the Gateway Masters event at Worthing's Beach House Park.

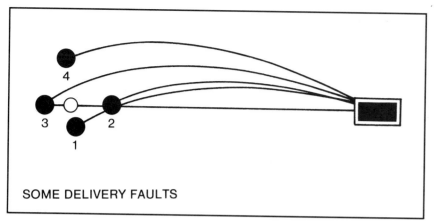

SOME DELIVERY FAULTS

DON'TS

1. Never throw the jack. Take your stance on the mat as if you are bowling a bowl and endeavour to bowl the jack to the distance at which you hope to obtain maximum advantage.

2. Don't run off the mat when delivering a bowl. Take your time.

3. Don't bowl narrow, as a slightly over-greened bowl is invariably better.

13. Take pride in building deep concentration and will power, but remember it is still only a game and do not let the result get out of perspective. Train yourself to think carefully about the game and in practice be prepared to experiment, as it is the only way to learn. Your tactics and general knowledge will then improve steadily.

14. Remember that few bowlers succeed in top-class play unless they have excellent temperaments. Set out to be an example to others on the green. Sportsmanship costs nothing. A player who is a true sportsman will always be an inspiration to his team-mates and the serenity and coolness that accompany him will be conducive to better play, with his partners being completely relaxed but still concentrating to the full.

Some delivery faults. *1. The grassline taken was too narrow and the bowl has therefore come to rest across the jack. Check the position of your feet on the mat, ensure you delivered the bowl cleanly and make sure that your follow-through is sufficient.*

2. The bowl has reached the centre of the rink but has stopped short of the jack. Make sure that the bowl leaves your hand smoothly and that you impart the right momentum through backswing and follow-through.

3. The right grassline has been chosen, but there was a little too much pace. Check that you do not take too long a step on delivery and that your forearm is not too high when going into the backswing.

4. The bowl has finished about jack high but your bowl is too wide of your target. You have, in fact, taken too wide a grassline so adjust the position of your feet to reduce the angle and make sure that on delivery your arm is fairly close to your side in both backswing and follow-through.

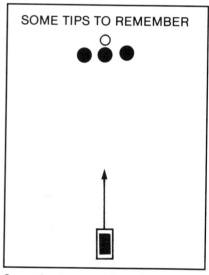

SOME TIPS TO REMEMBER

Some tips to remember. *1. You might think that these three bowls provide adequate protection for the jack, but your opposition will be able to clear them with a good running bowl.*

4. Don't allow your eyes to wander when bowling; keep them fixed on the shoulder of the intended arc and don't let yourself be distracted by shadow or movement. Wait until everything is still before you bowl.

5. Don't relax when you build up a big lead. There will surely come a time when you will regret it. Alternatively, never let your opponent think that he has disturbed you. Whatever the fortunes, appear serene and cheerful, and concentrate on how to pull those shots back and reverse the mental pressure.

6. Don't be too hasty in deciding which shot to play. Study the head carefully, for there are usually many more possibilities than are apparent at first glance, and don't fire unless you have examined the head and are absolutely sure that no alternative exists.

7. Don't let your opponent dictate the pace of the game. You cannot rush a game of bowls **and** give your best. You should play at your speed and let him play at his.

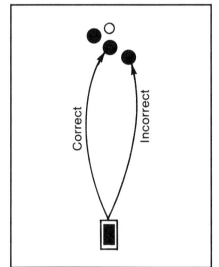

2. The forehand shot, for a right-handed player, may be a little difficult. A backhand onto the middle of the three bowls should provide the best opportunity for a shot.

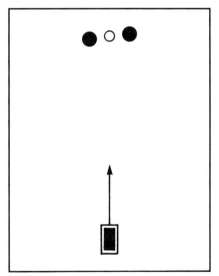

3. Here are two shots that any bowler should avoid, and which produce the 'jack high bowl'. Although they may be close to the jack, the bowls present your opposition with an easy chance to play to them for a shot. Avoid the temptation to drive and play a well greened draw shot.

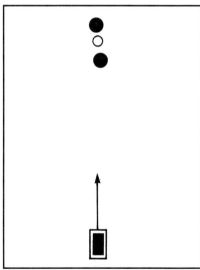

4. These two bowls are well-placed, giving a small target from the mat and covering the jack, which makes the length hard to determine. Only a good draw will win this end.

8 CONCENTRATION AND THE ART OF WINNING

Any aspiring bowler who wishes to become a champion must accumulate mental, tactical and technical skills. He will invariably become groomed first in the technical aspects of the game, while improving tactically through competitive experience. He then needs to learn some of the mental aspects of bowls. These include the right philosophical attitude to the game, the correct approach to winning and losing, mental toughness, courage, concentration and patience.

The first question to ask is 'Why do you play bowls?' Is it simply a form of relaxation, comradeship, a means to keep fit, or do you like to measure your capabilities against those of others?

All are good reasons for playing any sport, but they are not directly related to winning or losing. In serious tournament circles there are two groups of competitors. The first group consider that winning is not just important, it is everything, while the second receive their enjoyment from striving to be

Former English Bowling Association President, Fred Taylor of Cumbria (right), watches anxiously as a Somerset bowl approaches the head in this Middleton Cup semi-final at Worthing's Beach House Park.

better players through competition. For them the measurement of success is through beating supposedly superior players and so improving their standards. Winning, therefore, inspires them to strive for even higher achievements. Defeat will only galvanise them to examine their weaknesses and endeavour to put them right. They will show their opponents every respect, but will not believe it wrong to beat them by the best score possible. After all, it is surely a compliment to your opponent to put up your best performance at all times.

Some opponents will not thank you for showing any sympathy. Remember, until the last end has been played, or the target reached, you may still have a chance. As long as there is a mathematical probability, don't give up. Many a match has been won on the last end because an opponent imagined that he was enough in front to win and momentarily relaxed. Don't be frightened to beat someone 21–0; remember: he, too, is assessing his standard as a competitor.

Not wanting to lose is also a good attitude to adopt, as it will channel your aggression into playing at your best and will give you the mental toughness required to win against a worthy opponent.

Developing the right attitude and

approach to winning does not come overnight. It grows with self-discipline and a lot of practice on and off the green. As it sinks into your sub-conscious mind, the more freedom you will have to concentrate on successful play.

BE POSITIVE

What the bowler has to develop is the right attitude towards the fact that he can do nothing about any previous bowl, either one delivered by himself or by his opponent. He must concentrate on the next bowl to play. When his opponent's bowl comes to rest, he must analyse the situation, decide on his course of action and prepare to execute the shot.

Some players are capable of making mental pictures of the shot they want to play and go through it quickly in their minds. If you are convinced that your shot is going to be a winner, then you will create the right inner calmness needed to play it. You must be fully committed when you play your shot; a half-hearted approach will produce a half-hearted shot.

On the mat relax your body to ensure that your arms and legs are suitably loose. Line up your intended direction, ensure that you do not clutch your bowl and let it glide easily out of your hand. Let your arm follow rhythmically

The intense concentration needed to play a shot is perfectly illustrated here by the former World Indoor Singles Champion, Bob Sutherland.

through and use your head to control your balance. Remember that as a game progresses you will lose some of your mental aptitude. You will not be quite as alert by the twentieth end as you were on the first. That is the time when someone can slip through your guard. (It is a known fact that many goals in football are scored in the last ten minutes when a defender's mental edge is beginning to slip.)

Most bowlers seem to find it imperative to give their complete attention to every bowl that travels down the rink, suffering all the agonies and ecstasies of their opponents' bowls as well as their own. This is mentally very draining. You will find it better just to concentrate on your own problems. Many top players have the ability to turn from a 'passive' to an 'active' concentration. Some can even switch off completely until it is their turn to bowl; as long as a player does not lose sight of his objectives, who is to say that this approach is not right?

Positive attitudes, courage, concentration, the ability to harness nervousness, tactics and technical competence are vital to all games and will help take anyone to the top. Also vital to success are knowledge, determination, intelligence and patience to eliminate or reduce flaws.

THE HEAD

The various shots used in the game have been described in chapter 3 and you will quickly realise, particularly in the 'fours' game, that these shots need to be translated into the building of a 'head'.

In every game the 'head' is the area of the green where fortunes are won or lost. Any one bowl can swing the balance of power. This means that only general principles can be laid down, because it is difficult to stipulate hard and fast rules. Each 'head' will be different and a skip will call on a variety of shots and counter-measures to produce the result he is looking for. The tactics involved in building a 'head' will vary depending on the game being played—singles, pairs, triples or fours—but the range of shots available stays the same.

Singles

In bowls the twists of fortune seem to be more pronounced for the individual in a singles game than for members of a team; but whoever is experiencing a difficult time must be able to brush aside ill-fortune and concentrate on the next bowl. As each singles player has four bowls (although some singles matches, especially in the Federation game, are played with two bowls, as are all crown matches) the building up of a head can be followed closely: there is not quite the same 'clutter' that is experienced in other games.

The singles player must be a master of the draw shot, because this is the key shot of the game. If his first bowl is placed within inches

of the jack, then he will have taken the initiative. A bowl which obscures the jack from the view of an opponent is a bonus. His second bowl should be concentrated on drawing behind the jack and then the remaining two bowls can be used to counteract those of the opponent.

You should avoid putting bowls in 'jack-high' positions because these offer an opponent the ideal chance for resting to, or 'wicking' off. You should also avoid the tendency to 'pack' the jack because this will be too vulnerable a target for the firm bowl, and without cover at the back you could find a sudden conversion could easily rob you of your advantage. It is far better to ensure modest success by playing positional bowls either to prevent or to minimise the damage a firm shot could cause.

You could play a block shot short of the jack to finish in the path of a firm bowl, or a back bowl to counteract any backward movement of the jack. In general, the back bowl is easier to play and is often more profitable.

In singles the winner of an end has the choice of mat placement and jack length on the following end. Remember that a short jack on a fast green favours the better player and that as the speed of the green increases, so will the margin of error.

If you are on a winning length it is best not to alter your mat position, but if you are on the receiving end any experiment may be worth trying. However, all length planning will be of no avail if your jack delivery is inaccurate. So, make sure that you deliver the jack with the same accuracy that you deliver a bowl.

Pairs

The pairs game provides two players with the chance to consult with one another and to express the maximum degree of mutual confidence and knowledge of the game. It is an intimate partnership which has the advantage of providing both players with something to do throughout the whole game, either at the mat or directing the 'head'.

In the association game each player will use four bowls, and therefore the number in the 'head' doubles from that in singles play. The emphasis will switch from the drawing shots to a more varied selection with firmer bowls.

Accurate drawing will be supported by positional bowls, but attacking shots should also be coupled with defensive ones. Ideally, the lead should aim to get his first bowl on the jack and, if achieving that aim, should consolidate his position behind the jack. The skip should be able to go

to the mat with the knowledge that he has not got many worries. He should have a position that favours his best shots, which probably means the opposition will have to play shots that are not really to their liking.

Triples

While the draw shot is still of importance in triples, this factor decreases as the game progresses. The advantage of forceful play increases dramatically in the concluding stages of the triples game.

One of the biggest advantages from a player's point of view in the triples game is that, compared with rink play, he has an additional bowl to help towards his tactical plan.

Fours

The vast majority of bowls games will consist of team games involving four players—lead, no. 2, third and skip. The duties of these players are described elsewhere in the book, but it goes without saying that if four players can weld themselves into one unit and follow the same principle as did the 'Three Musketeers' ('All for one and one for all!'), they can be very effective.

Obviously different players will read a head in different ways, so it is often up to the skip to interpret

the advice given him and then to assess this with his own knowledge before making the decision on the choice of shot.

There are many points to consider during an end of bowls regarding the state of the head at any given time and the choice of shot(s) open to the player on the mat. Some basic questions can, however, be asked before making a decision on which shot to play.

The four questions that you should immediately ask yourself are:

What do I stand to gain out of playing the shot?

What do I stand to lose by playing the shot?

What are the chances of the shot working against me?

Is this the right time in the match to play such a shot?

You are therefore looking at the shot in the light of percentage advantages and disadvantages. There are many things that can happen: you may play the shot correctly, but on the other hand you may not execute the shot the way you intended.

You may decide to risk playing the shot anyway, despite the odds being slightly against you. You may also decide that because the game is at a crucial stage, it is best not to risk it. Look at the scoreboard before making your final decision. If you are playing in a team game, you must consider what effect your actions may have on your team-mates. Sometimes if you are going to take chances, it is best to do this in the early ends, when you can afford to drop a big count.

It is as well to remember that it is perhaps better to have three good shots in a position, which makes it more difficult for your opponent to get at the jack, than to have six shots in a position where your opponent can easily reach the jack.

Similarly, if you are one down but you have useful close bowls, it is sometimes better to accept the situation than to try to move the jack. Your opponent might have the better of the back bowls. If you have the advantage if the jack is moved, then naturally you would take the risk. But it so often happens that a skip tries to play for the jack, ends up taking his only bowl out of the head and goes from being just one down to several!

In the opening ends of a match, especially outdoors, you may be struggling to find a length and the green may be changing. So, it is probably best to concentrate on getting your drawing shots correct first while you find the pace of the green. Forget the running shots until you are confident that you can play them. This is why the trial ends are so important. They help you to find the line, even if you pick the wrong hand. At least if you have found the pace of the green you can then adjust.

When you are playing a game, particularly singles, remember that your first priority must be to concentrate on what you want to achieve, and not in trying to frustrate your opponent. However, that does not mean you must present him with easy targets. You must try to make his objectives more difficult to achieve.

Don't try the dramatic shot when the alternative, while not being as productive, is simpler. It is all a question of priorities and asking yourself those questions mentioned at the beginning of the section. Get the right strength for the shot, or use just a little extra weight, and you should succeed.

The following points are worth thinking about:

(a) There are a number of ways to save shots but the position of the bowls and their distance from the jack should always be the deciding factor. Just remember which is your main priority—saving or converting? Saving may be the easier shot. Careful study of the game and knowledge of the green should be considered.

(b) Don't lose sight of the order of play—who has to deliver the last bowl? If your opponent has the last bowl, look at the situation in the light of what he can achieve with it.

(c) Concentrate in the early stages of a match to perfect your line and find the pace of the green. Don't try too many running shots, as you may find the shots gap too big to recover from. Play tightly during the final ends and don't let a large shots gap in your favour lull you into a false sense of security.

(d) Weight is particularly important with the firm shots—wicks, wrests and plants. It is vital to study the effects of bowl on bowl so that you can get the right angles. Always remember that bowls act differently on slow and fast greens.

There is so much to learn, particularly on the opening ends of a match and especially if you are playing on an unfamiliar green. You will need to experiment for the first few ends in finding the best hands to bowl. Watch how your opponent's bowls behave—but don't always follow them because yours will not necessarily act in the same way.

And remember that if you are under pressure your three greatest allies will be: patience, concentration and, most important of all, common sense!

9 OTHER CODES

You should have no difficulty in finding a bowling green in your district, but what type of bowls is played there will largely depend on the area of the country in which you live. For example, outdoor bowls in England and North Wales falls into two main categories—level green and crown green. The level (or flat) green game is also played under two codes, Association and Federation. The Association game is the internationally recognised style of play and has more participants than any of the others. It is played exclusively in Scotland, Ireland, most of Wales, except the northern coast, and in all English counties except Cheshire and Staffordshire. The Federation game, which is played on level greens but with variations in the rules, is popular in the eastern counties, from Northumberland and Durham, down to Lincolnshire, Nottinghamshire, Derbyshire through to Norfolk and Suffolk. Humberside and Cleveland have recently joined this code.

Former English Bowling Association National Singles Champion, Tommy Buller of Durham, in action at Worthing.

It has often been said that crown green bowls evolved because there are no flat and level areas of land in the north-west of England, so it was necessary to devise a game of bowls that took this into account. Successive writers have failed to trace the origins and history of the crown code, but it is generally thought that it was introduced to give hazards that are impossible on a flat green. It is also a version of bowls that follows the 'roving' jack principle, as opposed to the level game played on specifically laid out rinks.

The Federation code, in modified forms, has been played for over a century and has its origins in the Northumberland and Durham Bowling Association of 1892. It is said that the game originated, using as its basis a two-bowl triples, because of the need to provide a short game for the northern and midland factory workers. As the greens did not need ditches and banks, it could be played on ordinary lawns, often those attached to public houses. Eventually, the Northumberland and Durham clubs joined with those playing the code in a Midlands and East Anglian Association, and this union ultimately resulted in 1954 in the retitling of the body as the English Bowling Federation.

England's dual indoor/outdoor international, Billy Hobart, was a former English Bowling Federation Champion before turning to the more popular association code.

CROWN GREEN BOWLS AND FLAT GREEN BOWLS

Crown green bowls differs from the flat green game in three important areas. The green itself rises from the edges to the centre anything from 15 to 45 cm (6 to 18″), and even more in some extreme cases, and there is basically no restriction on its dimensions. Most greens are about 120 square feet (40 yd × 40 yd) (11.15 m²), but there are many which are either bigger or smaller. The bowls and the jack vary from those used in the flat green game. The bowls are lighter and have a smaller bias, although there are no restrictions on either weight or bias as there are on flat green bowls which must conform to a standard 'bias three'. The jack in crown green bowls is, in effect, a miniature bowl, is biased and must conform to a set standard.

The other main difference is that the game is played on all parts of the green and not in conventional fixed rinks.

Bowls for all. The handicapped can derive great enjoyment from the sport. David Bryant helps some wheelchair players on a short mat.

INDOOR BOWLS

The rules governing indoor bowls are similar in nearly every respect to the outdoor ones, except that a heavier jack is used and strings are usually dispensed with. Due to the nature of the carpets, the game takes place up and down in one direction.

The indoor season normally begins on 1 October, although some stadiums open for their autumn and winter sessions a few weeks earlier, and some stay open during the summer to run small leagues for those who prefer not to chance the vagaries of the summer weather. Bowls is an easily packaged sport and this is one of the underlying reasons behind the spectacular growth of the indoor game. The purpose-built indoor greens offer pleasant and comfortable surroundings in which to play, regardless of weather conditions.

The addition of the short mat game and carpet bowls gives a further dimension to the indoor scene and allows many bowlers who cannot play at the larger indoor stadiums the chance to enjoy the sport. Target bowls, where players bowl to a circular, plastic-based mat, four feet in diameter, with scoring rings similar to those on an archery target, provides useful practice.

DUTIES OF A MARKER

Apart from the basic duties of the marker set out in Law 72 of the International Bowling Board's **Laws of the Game**, I cannot find any publication on this subject which helpfully enlarges on the duties required of the marker. I am, therefore, setting out each of the sub-sections of Law 72 and adding observations which in my opinion may prove helpful to those interested in this important aspect of the game.

Section A states that the marker shall control the game in accordance with the IBB basic laws. He shall, before play commences, examine all bowls for the imprint of the IBB stamp, or that of its national association (such imprint to be clearly visible), and shall ascertain by measurement the width of the rink of play.

Engineering calipers, such as the type seen here, are used for close measurements.

It is important that the marker shall unobtrusively impress upon the players that he is both capable and reliable, and to do this he should see that he is properly dressed, wearing a blazer and tie. His blazer may be of assistance to him for keeping equipment, the scorecard and a pencil in the pockets. He should also be in possession of a piece of chalk and a suitable measure, and should ensure that other equipment, such as a measuring tape (100 feet (30 metres)), long string measure (12 feet (3.6 metres) or more) and calipers are near at hand if required.

In **Section B** the marker is required to centre the jack, and place a full length jack 2 yards (1.84 metres) from the ditch.

He shall centre the jack at each end. If the jack in its original course comes to rest at a distance of less than 2 yards (1.84 metres) from the opposite ditch, it shall be moved out to that distance, ensuring that the side of the jack nearest to the mat is 2 yards (1.84 metres) from the front ditch. When doing so a glance down the rink is advisable to see that the mat has been placed on the centre-line of the rink. It may be helpful, if the manufacturer's name appears on the jack, to align it with this mark directly down the centre-line, which would give an indication should the jack be moved by a toucher.

Section C states that the marker shall ensure that the jack is not less than 25 yards (22.86 metres) from the front edge of the mat, after it has been centred.

The marker has the right to have the length of the jack measured if he wishes.

Section D states that the marker shall stand at one side of the rink, and to the rear of the jack.

It is suggested that the marker should retire to a position 6–9 feet behind the head and 5 or 6 feet on one side of the rink. If he alternates the side of the rink on which he stands, he will not always be obstructing the view of one section of spectators all the time. He should position himself to ensure that his shadow does not fall on the head.

A marker shall answer affirmatively or negatively a player's inquiry as to whether a bowl is jack high (**Section E**). If requested, he shall indicate the distance of any bowl from the jack or from any other bowl, and also, if requested, indicate which bowl he thinks is shot and/or the relative position of any other bowl.

If a question is asked and his answer is made incorrect by virtue of a bowl falling over, he should advise the player of the changed position, provided that the player has not yet delivered his bowl.

The marker should never volunteer information and should only answer questions from the player in possession of the mat. He should never invite players to come to the head to judge the position for themselves.

Section F Subject to contrary directions from either opponent under Law 34, he shall mark all touchers immediately they come to rest and shall remove chalk marks from non-touchers. With the agreement of both opponents he shall remove all dead bowls from the green and the ditch. He shall mark the positions of the jack and touchers which are in the ditch.

If, in the opinion of the marker, a toucher or a wrongly chalked bowl comes to rest in such a position that the act of making a chalk mark, or of erasing it, is likely to move the bowl or to alter the head, the bowl shall not be marked or have its mark erased but shall be 'indicated' as a toucher or non-toucher as the case may be. To avoid possible misunderstanding it is preferable to obtain consent from both opponents on these points before the commencement of play, and to have an understanding with the players to allow time for him to mark a toucher, or 'indicate' a toucher, before the next bowl is delivered.

The marker shall not move, or cause to be moved, either jack or bowls until each player has agreed to the number of shots (**Section G**).

Keep well clear of the head when the end has been completed, because the players determine the result of the end and advise the marker. If requested to measure, the marker should announce his decision to the players but he should never touch a bowl or jack, since this may disturb their position.

Section H The marker shall measure carefully all doubtful shots when requested by either player. If unable to come to a decision which is satisfactory to the players, he shall call in an umpire. If an official umpire has not been appointed, the marker shall select one. **The decision of the umpire shall be final.**

When measuring at the request of one of the players the marker should be careful to measure from the nearest point of the jack to the nearest point of the bowls. The measurement should be taken from the jack to bowl A, to bowl B, and then again to bowl A to ensure that the measure has not slipped, and to confirm that the first measurement was accurate.

Section I The marker shall enter the score at each end, and shall intimate to the players the state of the game. When the game is finished he shall see that the score card, containing the names of the players, is signed by the players and disposed of in accordance with the rules of the competition.

If an official umpire has been appointed it is preferable to hand the completed score card to him.

Finally, here are a few general observations which are intended to be of guidance to the marker:

1. It is not advisable to talk to the players or spectators as this will inevitably result in them talking to the marker, which in turn could interfere with the concentration of the bowlers.

2. Remember that the marker is always impartial and he should never applaud a good shot.

3. Keep your chalk in your hand or pocket and do not fiddle with it.

4. Keep your blazer buttoned and see that your tie does not flap about.

5. Stand perfectly still while play is in progress, always watching for a signal from the player in possession of the mat, and keep alert to observe and mark any touchers.

6. Be careful to ensure that you do nothing which may break the players' concentration.

John R. Carr
Hon. Secretary
English Bowls Umpires Association

RULES AND LIST OF BOWLS SIZES

To enjoy bowls fully all bowlers should be conversant with the laws of the game. After all, it is these laws that form the basis of your sport.

The earliest known laws were drawn up by King Charles II, the Duke of York and the Duke of Buckingham in 1670, and that framework still remains today. However, it was not until 1849 that a complete Code of Laws was drawn up by clubs in the west of Scotland under the direction of Wm. Mitchell, a Glasgow solicitor and keen bowler.

Mitchell's laws were adopted by all clubs in the west of Scotland and later by the Scottish Bowling Association when it was formed in 1893. Later still, in 1905, the International Bowling Board was formed and this, too, adopted the Scottish BA laws.

The laws of flat green bowls in all parts of the world are largely founded on those that Mitchell drafted and issued in 1849. (Current laws are printed here by

kind permission of the IBB.) There are some variations to these laws. For example, the English Bowling Federation code, which is used in eleven counties covering East Anglia, East Midlands and the North, has five basic differences from the IBB laws:

1. There are no 'touchers' (therefore, any bowl that goes into the ditch is 'dead', although if the jack goes into the ditch it remains 'live').

2. Only bowls within 6 feet (1.8 metres) of the jack can be counted for shots.

3. Players may alter the order in which they play after each complete end.

4. In rink play, three players constitute a rink.

5. The mat may be moved up to 12 feet (3.6 metres) from the front edge of the ditch.

It has often been said that crown green bowls evolved because there were no level areas of land in the north-west of England. In fact, no

one seems sure how the 'crown' idea developed. The green rises from the edges to the centre from 6 to 18 inches (15–46 cm), more in extreme cases, and play is directed all over the green and not in rinks.

There are also variations in the pairs game, particularly in Australia. Here the lead bowls two bowls, followed by the skip; then they change over and the lead delivers his final two, with the skips finishing the game. The advantage of this is that it generally calls for a wider variety of shots from each player.

The following selection of Laws of bowls, as formulated by the International Bowling Board, are reproduced by kind permission of the English Bowling Association. (It should be appreciated that no code of laws governing a game has yet achieved such perfection as to cope with every situation. The code of laws governing bowls is no exception. Unusual incidents not definitely provided for in the laws frequently occur. It is well, therefore, to remember that the laws have been framed in the belief that true sportsmanship will prevail: that in the absence of any express rule common sense will find a way to complete a happy solution to a knotty problem.)

Definitions

1. (a) 'Controlling Body' means the body having immediate control of the conditions under which a match is played. The order shall be:

(i) The International Bowling Board,

(ii) The National Bowling Association,

(iii) The State, Division, Local District or County Association,

(iv) The Club on whose Green the Match is played.

(B) 'Skip' means the Player, who, for the time being, is in charge of the head on behalf of the team.

(c) 'Team' means either a four, a triples or a pair.

(d) 'Side' means any agreed number of Teams, whose combined scores determine the results of the match.

(e) 'Four' means a team of four players whose positions in order of playing are named, Lead, Second, Third, Skip.

(f) 'Bowl in Course' means a bowl from the time of its delivery until it comes to rest.

(g) 'End' means the playing of the Jack and all the bowls of all the opponents in the same direction on a rink.

(h) 'Head' means the Jack and such bowls as have come to rest within the boundary of the rink and are not dead.

(i) 'Mat Line' means the edge of the Mat which is nearest to the front ditch. From the centre of the Mat Line all necessary measurements to Jack or bowls shall be taken.

(j) 'Master Bowl' means a bowl which has been approved by the I.B.B. as having the minimum bias required, as well as in all other respects complying with the Laws of the Game and is engraved with the words 'Master Bowl'.

(i) A Standard Bowl of the same bias as the Master Bowl shall be kept in the custody of each National Association.

(ii) A Standard Bowl shall be provided for the use of each official Licensed Tester.

(k) 'Jack High' means that the nearest portion of the Bowl referred to is in line with and at the same distance from the Mat Line as the nearest portion of the Jack.

(l) 'Pace of Green' means the number of seconds taken by a bowl from the time of its delivery to the moment it comes to rest, approximately 30 yards (27.43 metres) from the Mat Line.

(m) 'Displaced' as applied to a Jack or Bowl means 'disturbed' by any agency that is not sanctioned by these laws.

(n) A 'set of bowls' means four bowls all of which are the same manufacture, and are of the same size, weight, colour and serial number where applicable.

13. Play arrangements Games shall be organised in the following play arrangements:

(a) As a single game.

(b) As a team game.

(c) As a sides game.

(d) As a series of single games, team games, or side games.

(e) As a special tournament of games.

14. A single game shall be played on one rink of a Green as a single-handed game by two contending players, each playing two, three or four bowls singly and alternately.

15. (a) A pairs game by two contending teams of two players called lead and skip according to the order in which they play, and who at each end shall play four bowls alternately, the leads first, then the skips similarly.

(For other than International and Commonwealth Games, players in a pairs game may play two, three or four bowls each, as previously arranged by the Controlling Body.)

(b) A pairs game by two contending teams of two players called Lead and Skip according to the order in which they play, and who at each end shall play four bowls and may play alternatively in the following order: Lead 2 bowls, Skip 2 bowls, then repeat this order of play.

16. A triples game by two contending teams of three players, who shall play two or three bowls singly and in turn, the leads playing first.

17. A fours game by two contending teams of four players, each member playing two bowls singly and in turn.

18. A side game shall be played by two contending sides, each composed of an equal number of teams/players.

Starting the game
23. (a) **Trial ends** Before start of play in any competition, match or game, or on the resumption of an unfinished competition, match or game on another day, not more than one trial end each way shall be played.
(b) **Tossing for opening play** The captains in a side game or skips in a team shall toss to decide which side or team shall play first, but in all singles games the opponents shall toss, the winner of the toss to have the option of decision. In the event of a tied (no score) or a dead end, the first to play in the tied end or dead end shall again play first.
In all ends subsequent to the first the winner of the preceding scoring end shall play first.

27. Stance on mat A player shall take his stance on the mat, and at the moment of delivering the Jack or his Bowl, shall have one foot remaining entirely within the confines of the mat. The foot may be either in contact with, or over, the mat. Failure to observe this law constitutes foot-faulting.

28. Foot-faulting Should a player infringe the Law of foot-faulting the Umpire may, after having given a warning, have the bowl stopped and declared dead. If the bowl has disturbed the head, the opponent shall have the option of either resetting the head, leaving the head as altered or declaring the end dead.

30. Jack improperly delivered
Should the Jack in any end be not delivered from a proper stance on the mat, or if it ends its original course in the ditch or outside the side boundary of the rink, or less than 70 feet (21.35 metres) in a straight line of play from the front edge of the mat, it shall be returned and the opposing player shall deliver the Jack but shall not play first.
The Jack shall be returned if it is improperly delivered, but the right of the player first delivering the Jack in that end, to play the first bowl of the end shall not be affected.
No player shall be permitted to challenge the legality of the original length of the Jack after

each player in a singles game or leads in a team game have each bowled one bowl.

Movement of bowls
32. 'Live' bowl A Bowl which, in its original course on the Green, comes to rest within the boundaries of the rink, and not less than 15 yards (13.71 metres) from the front edge of the mat, shall be accounted as a 'Live' bowl and shall be in play.

33. 'Touchers' A bowl which, in its original course on the green, touches the Jack, even though such bowl passes into the ditch within the boundaries of the rink, shall be counted as a 'live' bowl and shall be called a 'toucher'. If after having come to rest a bowl falls over and touches the Jack before the next succeeding bowl is delivered, or if in the case of the last bowl of an end it falls and touches the Jack within the period of half a minute invoked under Law 53, such bowl shall also be a 'toucher'. No bowl shall be accounted a 'toucher' by playing on to, or by coming into contact with, the Jack while the Jack is in the ditch. If a 'toucher' in the ditch cannot be seen from the mat its position may be marked by a white or coloured peg about 2 inches (51 mm) broad placed upright on the top of the bank and immediately in line with the place where the 'toucher' rests.

34. Marking a 'toucher' A 'toucher' shall be clearly marked with a chalk mark by a member of the player's team. If, in the opinion of either Skip, or opponent in Singles, a 'toucher' or a wrongly chalked bowl comes to rest in such a position that the act of making a chalk mark, or of erasing it, is likely to move the bowl or to alter the head, the bowl shall not be marked or have its mark erased but shall be 'indicated' as a 'toucher' or 'non-toucher' as the case may be. If a bowl is not so marked or not so 'indicated' before the succeeding bowl comes to rest it ceases to be a 'toucher'. If both Skips or opponents agree that any subsequent movement of the bowl eliminates the necessity for continuation of the 'indicated' provision the bowl shall thereupon be marked or have the chalk mark erased as the case may be. Care should be taken to remove 'toucher' marks from all bowls before they are played, but should a player fail to do so, and should the bowl not become a 'toucher' in the end in play, the marks shall be removed by the opposing Skip or his deputy or marker immediately the bowl comes to rest unless the bowl is 'indicated' as a 'non-toucher' in circumstances governed by earlier provisions of this Law.

35. Movement of 'touchers' A 'toucher' in play in the ditch may be moved by the impact of a jack in play or of another 'toucher' in play, and also by the impact of a non-toucher which remains in play after the impact, and any movement of the 'toucher' by such incidents shall be valid. However, should the non-toucher enter the ditch at any time after the impact, it shall be dead, and the 'toucher' shall be deemed to have been displaced by a dead bowl and the provisions of Law 38(e) shall apply.

36. Bowl accounted 'dead'
(a) Without limiting the application of any other of these Laws, a bowl shall be accounted dead if it:

(i) not being a 'toucher', comes to rest in the ditch or rebounds on to the playing surface of the rink after contact with the bank or with the Jack or a 'toucher' in the ditch, or

(ii) after completing its original course, or after being moved as a result of play, it comes to rest wholly outside the boundaries of the playing surface of the rink, or within 15 yards (13.71 metres) of the front of the mat, or

(iii) in its original course, passes beyond a side boundary of the rink on a bias which would prevent its re-entering the rink. (A bowl is not rendered 'dead' by a player carrying it whilst inspecting the head.)
(b) Skips, or Opponents in Singles, shall agree on the question as to whether or not a bowl is 'dead', and having reached agreement, the question shall not later be subject to appeal to the Umpire. Any member of either team may request a decision from the Skips but no member shall remove any bowl prior to the agreement of the Skips. If Skips or Opponents are unable to reach agreement as to whether or not a bowl is 'dead' the matter shall be referred to the Umpire.

37. Bowl rebounding Only 'Touchers' rebounding from the face of the bank to the ditch or to the rink shall remain in play.

38. Bowl displacement
(a) Displacement by rebounding 'non-toucher'—bowl displaced by a 'non-toucher' rebounding from the bank shall be restored as near as possible to its original position, by a member of the opposing team.
(b) Displacement by participating player—if a bowl, while in motion or at rest on the green, or a 'toucher' in the ditch, be interfered with, or displaced by one of the players, the opposing skip shall have the option of:

(i) restoring the bowl as near as possible to its original position;

(ii) letting it remain where it rests;

(iii) declaring the bowl 'dead';

(iv) or declaring the end dead.
(c) Displacement by a neutral object or neutral person (other than as provided in Clause (d) hereof):

(i) of a bowl in its original

course—if such a bowl be displaced within the boundaries of the rink of play without having disturbed the head, it shall be replayed. If it be displaced and it has disturbed the head, the skips, or the opponents in singles, shall reach agreement on the final position of the displaced bowl and on the replacement of the head, otherwise the end shall be dead. These provisions shall also apply to a bowl in its original course displaced outside the boundaries of the rink of play provided such bowl was running on a bias which would have enabled it to re-enter the rink.

(ii) of a bowl at rest, or in motion as a result of play after being at rest—if such a bowl be displaced, the skips, or opponents in singles, shall come to an agreement as to the position of the bowl and of the replacement of any part of the head disturbed by the displaced bowl, otherwise the end shall be dead.

(d) Displacement inadvertently produced—if a bowl be moved at the time of it being marked or measured it shall be restored to its former position by an opponent. If such displacement is caused by a Marker or an Umpire, the Marker or Umpire shall replace the bowl.

(e) Displacement by dead bowl—if a 'toucher' in the ditch be displaced by a dead bowl from the rink of play, it shall be restored to its original position by a player of the opposite team or by the marker.

39. 'Line bowls' A bowl shall not be accounted as outside any circle or line unless it be entirely clear of it. This shall be ascertained by looking perpendicularly down upon the bowl or by placing a square on the green.

Movement of jack
40. A 'live' jack in the ditch
A Jack moved by a bowl in play into the front ditch within the boundaries of the rink shall be deemed to be 'live'. It may be moved by the impact of a 'toucher' in play and also by the impact of a 'non-toucher' which remains in play after the impact; any movement of the Jack by such incidents shall be valid. However, should the 'non-toucher' enter the ditch after impact, it shall be 'dead' and the Jack shall be deemed to have been 'displaced' by a 'dead' bowl and the provisions of Law 48 shall apply. If the Jack in the ditch cannot be seen from the mat its position shall be marked by a 'white' peg about 2 inches (51 mm) broad and not more than 4 inches (102 mm) in height, placed upright on top of the bank and immediately in line from the place where the Jack rests.

41. A jack accounted 'dead'
Should the Jack be driven by a bowl in play and come to rest wholly beyond the boundary of the rink, i.e., over the bank, or over the side boundary, or into any opening or inequality of any kind in the bank, or rebound to a distance less than 61 feet (18.59 metres) in direct line from the centre of the front edge of the mat to the Jack in its rebounded position, it shall be accounted 'dead'. ('National Associations have the option to vary the distance to which a Jack may rebound and still be playable for games other than International and Commonwealth Games.')

42. 'Dead' end When the Jack is 'dead' the end shall be regarded as a 'dead' end and shall not be accounted as a played end even though all the bowls in that end have been played. All 'dead' ends shall be played anew in the same direction unless both Skips or Opponents in Singles agree to play in the opposite direction. After a 'dead' end situation, the right to deliver the jack shall always return to the player who delivered the original jack.

43. Playing to a boundary jack
The Jack, if driven to the side boundary of the rink and not wholly beyond its limits, may be played to on either hand and, if necessary, a bowl may pass outside the side limits of the rink. A bowl so played, which comes to

rest within the boundaries of the rink, shall not be accounted 'dead'. If the Jack be driven to the side boundary line and comes to rest partly within the limits of the rink, a bowl played outside the limits of the rink and coming to rest entirely outside the boundary line, even though it has made contact with the jack, shall be accounted 'dead' and shall be removed to the bank by a member of the player's team.

44. A damaged jack In the event of a jack being damaged, the Umpire shall decide if another jack is necessary and, if so, the end shall be regarded as a 'dead' end and another jack shall be substituted and the end shall be replayed anew.

45. A rebounding jack If the jack is driven against the face of the bank and rebounds on to the rink, or after being played into the ditch, it be operated on by a 'toucher', so as to find its way on to the rink, it shall be played to in the same manner as if it had never left the rink.

46. Jack displacement
(a) By a player
If the jack be diverted from its course while in motion on the green, or displaced while at rest on the green, or in the ditch, by any one of the players, the opposing skip shall have the jack restored to its former position, or allow it to remain where it rests and play the

end to a finish, or declare the end 'dead'.
(b) Inadvertently produced
If the jack be moved at the time of measuring by a player it shall be restored to its former position by an opponent.

47. Jack displaced by non-player
(a) If the jack, whether in motion or at rest on the rink, or in the ditch, be displaced by a bowl from another rink, or by any object or by an individual not a member of the team, the two skips shall decide as to its original position, and if they are unable to agree, the end shall be declared 'dead'.
(b) If a jack be displaced by a marker or umpire it shall be restored by him to its original position of which he shall be the sole judge.

48. Jack displaced by 'non-toucher' A jack displaced in the rink of play by a 'non-toucher' rebounding from the bank shall be restored, or as near as possible, to its original position by a player of the opposing team. Should a jack, however, after having been played into the ditch, be displaced by a 'dead bowl' it shall be restored to its marked position by a player of the opposing side or by the marker.

Fours play
The basis of the Game of Bowls is Fours Play.

49. The rink and fours play
(a) Designation of players. A team shall consist of four players, named respectively, lead, second, third and skip, according to the order in which they play, each playing two bowls.
(b) Order of Play. The leads shall play their two bowls alternately, and so on, each pair of players in succession to the end. No one shall play until his opponents' bowl shall have come to rest. Except under circumstances provided for in Law 63, the order of play shall not be changed after the first end has been played, under penalty of disqualification, such penalty involving the forfeiture of the match or game to the opposing team.

50. Possession of the rink
Possession of the rink shall belong to the team whose bowl is being played. The players in possession of the rink for the time being, shall not be interfered with, annoyed, or have their attention distracted in any way by their opponents. As soon as each bowl shall have come to rest, possession of the rink shall be transferred to the other team, time being allowed for marking a 'toucher'.

51. Position of players Players of each team not in the act of playing or controlling play, shall stand behind the jack and away from the head, or one yard (92 cm) behind the mat. As soon as the bowl is delivered, the skip or player directing, if in front of the jack shall retire behind it.

Result of end

53. 'The shot' A shot or shots shall be adjudged by the bowl or bowls nearer to the jack than any bowl played by the opposing player or players.

When the last bowl has come to rest, half a minute shall elapse, if either team desires, before the shots are counted.

Neither jack nor bowls shall be moved until each skip has agreed to the number of shots, except in circumstances where a bowl has to be moved to allow the measuring of another bowl.

54. Measuring conditions to be observed No measuring shall be allowed until the end has been completed.

All measurements shall be made to the nearest point of each object. If a bowl requiring to be measured is resting on another bowl which prevents its measurement, the best available means shall be taken to secure its position, whereupon the other bowl shall be removed. The same course shall be followed where more than two bowls are involved, or where, in the course of measuring, a single bowl is in danger of falling or otherwise changing its position. When it is necessary to measure to a bowl or jack in the ditch, and another bowl or jack on the green, the measurement shall be made with the ordinary flexible measure. Calipers may be used to determine the shot only when the bowls in question and the jack are on the same plane.

55. 'Tie'—no shot When at the conclusion of play in any end the nearest bowl of each team is touching the jack, or is deemed to be equidistant from the jack, there shall be no score recorded. The end shall be declared 'drawn' and shall be counted a played end.

56. Nothing in these Laws shall be deemed to make it mandatory for the last player to play his last bowl in any end, but he shall declare to his opponent or opposing skip his intention to refrain from playing it before the commencement of determining the result of the end and this declaration shall be irrevocable.

61. Play irregularities

(a) **Playing out of turn.** When a player has played before his turn the opposing skip shall have the right to stop the bowl in its course and it shall be played in its proper turn, but in the event of the bowl so played, having moved or displaced the jack or bowl, the opposing skip shall have the option of allowing the end to remain as it is after the bowl so played has come to rest, or having the end declared 'dead'.

(b) **Playing the wrong bowl.** A bowl played by mistake shall be replaced by the player's own bowl.

(c) **Changing bowls.** A player shall not be allowed to change his bowls during the course of a game, or in a resumed game, unless they be objected to, as provided in Law 9(c), or when a bowl has been so damaged in the course of play as, in the opinion of the Umpire, to render the bowl (or bowls) unfit for play.

(d) **Omitting to play**

(i) If the result of an end has been agreed upon, or the head has been touched in the agreed process of determining the result, then a player who forfeits or has omitted to play a bowl shall forfeit the right to play it.

(ii) A player who has neglected to play a bowl in the proper sequence shall forfeit the right to play such bowl, if a bowl has been played by each team before such mistake was discovered.

(iii) If before the mistake is noticed, a bowl has been delivered in the reversed order and the head has not been disturbed, the opponent shall then play two successive bowls to restore the correct sequence.

If the head has been disturbed Clause 61(a) shall apply.

Metric equivalents In connection with the manufacture of Bowls there is no objection to manufacturers using metric equivalents in lieu of the present figures, always provided that Law 9 of the Board's Laws is complied with. Furthermore, there is no objection to manufacturers indicating various sizes of Bowls by numerals, and the manufacturers will be entitled to use the following table if they so desire.

Size in inches	Size Number	Actual Metric (mm)	May be rounded off Metric (mm)
4-5/8	0	117.4	117
4-3/4	1	120.7	121
4-13/16	2	122.2	122
4-7/8	3	123.8	124
4-15/16	4	125.4	125
5	5	127.0	127
5-1/16	6	128.6	129
5-1/8	7	130.2	130

If size numbers are utilised and size measurements omitted, then no Bowl in diameter shall be less than 4-5/8 inches (117.4 mm) nor more than 5-1/8 inches (130.2 mm) and no Bowl shall weigh more than 3 lb 8 oz (1.59 kg).

GLOSSARY OF TERMS

Absolute – a bowl that draws the shot when other bowls are close to the jack.

Amateur – a player who has not competed for a monetary consideration or declared wager. Prizes won must have been taken in kind and not in cash.

Back bowl – a bowl some distance behind the jack.

Backhand – the delivery of a right-handed bowler towards the jack in a left-handed direction from the mat with bias inwards; or by a left-handed bowler in a right-handed direction with bias inwards.

Badge – a metal lapel badge or cloth blazer badge issued by a club, association, council or board and bearing an appropriate design and lettering.

Badged player – one who has represented his county or country or other equivalent association, or one who has played in an international trial game and is entitled to wear the appropriate cloth badge on his blazer.

Bank – the outer wall of the ditch above the level of the surface of the green.

Be up – to reach jack length with your bowls, and not be short.

Bias – the tendency of a bowl or other spheroid to divert from a straight line in movement because of an imbalance built in by shaping.

Block or guard – a bowl resting in the draw or near the centre-line to hinder an opponent in drawing the shot on a

particular hand or 'firing' at the jack or at a bowl or bowls in the head.

Bumper – a bowler allowing his bowl to drop onto the green, thereby causing damage to the surface.

Burned – a term used when the jack or a bowl has been interfered with or displaced other than by a bowl in play.

Cannon – a bowl which glances off one bowl onto another.

Chalked – when a 'toucher' has been chalked with a cross.

Clean sheet – a player who fails to score is said to have a clean plate or clean sheet.

Cot – colloquial term for the jack.

Count – the total of all the scoring bowls at the completion of an end.

Counter – a bowl conceded as a shot.

Covered – when the jack or a bowl is guarded by another bowl in front.

Dead bowl – a bowl which is no longer part of the head. A bowl illegally played.

Dead draw – a precise draw to the jack.

Dead end – an end which is deemed not to have been played. It can be caused by the jack being driven out of bounds and by certain accidental happenings.

Dead jack – an expression used when the jack has been driven by a bowl in play wholly beyond the boundary of the rink.

Dead length – an exact length drawn by a bowl to the jack or level with it.

Delivery – the releasing of the bowl from the hand onto the green.

Disc – the round piece of plastic, ivory or other material fitted into each side of the bowl, the smaller disc indicating the bias side.

Ditch – the channel no less than 2 inches deep (nor more than 8 inches) surrounding a flat green having as its inner boundary the face of the plinth, and as its outer boundary the outer wall up to the surface level of the green.

Ditcher – a bowl which runs into the ditch without touching the jack.

Draw – the effect of bias upon the bowl. The path which the bowl should take when approaching the jack allowing for the effect of the bias.

Drive – a bowl delivered forcefully with the object of breaking up the head, taking out the jack or a bowl or bowls, running the jack into the ditch, or causing a dead end.

Easy-running green – a medium paced green.

Either hand – the choice given to a bowler by his skip of playing the shot on either the backhand or the forehand.

End – playing to the jack all the bowls of all players once in the same direction on a rink.

End rink – the nearest rink to the ditch on each side of the green.

Extra end – an extra end is played by each rink in a tied match where a definite winner is required. A match of 21 ends finishing as a tie would thus be decided on the points scored in the 22nd end. If the match is still tied, further extra ends are played until a result is achieved.

Fast green – a green made fast by the sun, cutting close and rolling. A bowl takes a wider curve and longer course to the jack on a fast green.

Firing – delivering a bowl powerfully with the object of displacing the jack or a bowl or bowls.

Firm shot – a bowl played with more strength than is required for a dead draw, but with less than is required for the drive or firing shot.

Follow-on – a bowl played with enough force to move out of the way bowls in front of the jack and then continue on to the jack or other position desired.

Follow-through – fully completing the action of delivering the bowl along the line of delivery.

Foot-faulting – under International Bowling Board rules a bowler foot-faults unless he has at least one foot entirely within or over the confines of the mat at the moment of delivery.

Forcing shot – a strong delivery mid-way between a running bowls and firing shot in strength.

Forehand – the delivery of a right-handed bowler towards the jack in a right-hand direction from the mat; or by a left-handed bowler in a left-handed direction.

Four – a team of four players each with two bowls. In a match the leaders play their two bowls alternately, then the seconds, the thirds, and finally the skips.

Good length – a bowl resting at the desired length.

Hand – the path from mat to jack, forehand on the right, backhand on the left for right-handed bowlers, vice versa for left-handed bowlers.

Hatful – the maximum possible score in any one end—4 in singles, 8 in pairs or fours, and 9 in triples.

Head – the jack and so many of the bowls, whether on the rink or in the ditch, as have been played at any particular stage of any end.

Heavy – a bowl delivered with too much force for the shot required.

Heavy green – a slow green caused by rain, lack of rolling, or the grass not being cut closely.

Jack – the small ball used as a mark to play to. In crown green bowls the jack is biased.

Jack-high – when the bowl is level with the jack.

Kill an end – to cause a dead end by driving the jack out of the rink.

Kiss – a bowl just touching the jack.

Kitty – a colloquial term for the jack.

Land – the amount of green to take to allow the biased bowl to finish near the position desired.

Lead – the first player in a pairs, triples or rink who should lay the mat, roll the jack and draw the shot. In crown green bowls called the leader.

Lignum vitae – the name of the timber used for the manufacture of wooden bowls.

Linen thread – used to define the boundary of a rink and drawn tightly along the surface of the green. Fastened at each end of the green to the green boundary pins.

Live bowl – any bowl played and forming part of the head within the confines of the rink or any bowl in the ditch that has been chalked as a toucher.

Marker – the scorer in a singles match. The second player should record the score in a rink game.

Mat – the rectangular piece of material, usually rubber or canvas, used at each end to bowl from. The dimensions differ in various countries.

Match – a game between two opponents or teams to finish when an agreed number of ends have been played, or a fixed number of shots have been scored by either party.

Measure – a device employed to measure the distance from bowls to the jack to determine the shot.

Measurer – the player responsible for measuring.

Merry – describes a bowl which is running too fast.

Middle man – the second player in triples.

Narrow – used of a bowl which is played with too little green to allow for the effect of the bias and which finishes running away from the jack.

No score – a term used when the nearest bowl of each player in a singles, or the nearest bowl of each team in pairs, triples or rinks is equidistant from the jack.

Open hand – the side of the jack which has no bowls on it, or few compared with the other side.

Open jack – a jack in full view from the mat and not obstructed by bowls.

Opening the head – scattering bowls grouped in front of the jack so opening a channel to give an opportunity to draw the shot.

Pairing – when one of your bowls and one of your opponent's bowls are resting together at the head.

Pairs – two players constitute a team. They are the lead and the skip. A pairs match is played in various ways, each player having two, three, or four bowls— the lead playing his bowls alternately before the skips play theirs.

Peels – a Scottish expression to indicate that the scores are equal.

Pinching a bowl – bowling narrow.

Point of aim – the mark on the green, on the bank or behind the bank at which the player aims his bowl to allow the bias to curve it into the jack.

Port – a narrow passage between bowls through which to draw the shot.

Possession of the rink – applies from the time a player steps on to the mat until his bowl comes to rest.

Professional – a bowler who plays for money or a declared wager.

Protective sheets – large canvas sheets used to protect the ends of the rinks when the ground is wet. They are secured to the green and the bowl is delivered from a mat placed on the protective sheet or touching the back end of it.

Pulling a bowl – delivering a narrow bowl by pulling the hand across the body instead of following through.

Resting on a bowl – a bowl lying against an opposition bowl.

Rink – the rectangular space on a flat green between the boundary rods upon which play is confined.

Round robin – a competition in which each player meets all others. Also known as 'American Tournament'.

Rub – a term used when a bowl is diverted from its line of passage by some obstacle on or in the green.

Running wood – a bowl delivered with sufficient power to remove a target bowl before running on to a pre-determined position.

Scoring – recording on the score-cards and on the score-boards the shots as determined by the opponents in a singles, the lead in a pairs, and the second player in a triples or rink.

Second – the second player in a rink, who has the duty of recording the scores each end on the score-card, and each alternate end on the score-board.

Short – a bowl not up to the jack.

Short end – a throw of the jack to a minimum distance of 75 feet.

Shot – the nearest bowl to the jack.

Shots – the number of bowls of one singles player or team nearest to the jack.

Singles – a game between two players, usually with four bowls each, but sometimes with two bowls each.

Skip or skipper – the captain of a team.

Skittling – breaking up the head with a powerful drive.

Springing the jack – playing a bowl gently on to a 'shot' bowl which is touching the jack at the back of it, so that the contact will spring the jack forward a short distance.

Strong, too – when a bowl overruns the jack.

Take-out – a bowl which takes out an opponents scoring bowl, normally to capture the shot or shots.

Taking the green – allowing the bias to operate to the full extent so that the bowl on a correct length finishes on the correct line.

Third man – the third man in a rink who should do the measuring, determine the number of shots and take charge at the head when his skip is at the mat.

Toucher – a bowl in play which touches the jack (but not a bowl onto which the jack is played) or which, having ceased to run, falls over and touches the jack before the next bowl has been delivered. It remains in play throughout the end even when in the ditch. A toucher bowl is indicated by chalking a cross on it. If the chalk mark is not on the bowl before the next bowl comes to rest, the bowl which touched the jack is no longer a toucher.

Trailing – an expression used when a bowl moves the jack from an opposing bowl or on to a new position, the bowl keeping with the jack.

Trial end – in the International Bowling Board Laws of the Game, one trial (practice) end in each direction is allowed.

Triples – a team of three players each with three bowls. The leads play their three bowls alternately, then the number two players, and finally the skips.

Tuck in – an expression used when the jack is behind bowls and not visible from the mat.

Umpire – a person appointed by the controlling body or by the opponents to adjudicate on any question or dispute which may arise in the course of a game or on the question of whether the elements permit a game to start or continue.

Weight of the green – the force necessary to deliver a bowl of normal length having regard to the pace of the green.

Wick – an expression derived from curling, meaning a shot played onto another bowl and being thus deflected towards the jack.

Wide – when too much allowance for the bias has been made, and the bowl finishes wide of the jack.

Woods – a term used for bowls, derived from the fact that bowls were always made of wood before the advent of the composition bowl. The lignum vitae (wooden) bowl is extensively used in the British Isles, where bowlers still tend to call all types of bowl 'woods'.

Wrong bias – a bowl delivered with the bias side opposite to that intended.

Yard on shot – delivered with the object of pushing out an opponent's bowl resting near the jack or railing the jack away from it a yard or so.

INDEX